The Entrepreneur's Essential Roadmap – Take Your Business from 0 to 7-Figures in Record Time

by Christine Perakis, Esq.

COPYRIGHT AND DISCLAIMER

DEDICATION

I dedicate this book to my clients of the last 25 years, who have shown vision, courage, daring, dedication, loyalty, and an adventurous spirit taking on the challenges and joys of realizing their dream of running a business and not going it alone. Thank you for your trust in allowing me to be your navigator through the sometimes choppy seas of business life!

To Your Success,

Christine Perakis

CONTENTS

INTRODUCTION

Congratulations on taking this important step in your quest to grow your business and marketing skills!

By making a commitment to your business's growth, you will create more profits, more ease and more freedom for your life and business.

In contemplating this book and working with clients for so many years in so many different industries, I found that I have accumulated an enormous amount of useful marketing material that I've used for decades. This experience is drawn from working with, in and for many different business entities and senior leaders. Some of these businesses I created for and with clients and partners, as well as on my own, often from the ground up, turning them into multi-million dollar enterprises.

My roles have been diverse in a variety of environments. I've worked as an attorney for a large NY law firm and in private practice. I've done business with clients and companies all over the world, closed millions of dollars of financing from a variety of sources, been involved in movie production, finance and distribution, owned and managed a variety of small businesses including, among other industries, business consulting, entertainment, market research, competition go-karting, real estate portfolio management, personal growth and professional development, and multiple E-Commerce businesses. Several of these I continue to own and consult from outside the C-Suite. The strategies that I talk about in this book have been used throughout years and myriad enterprises, and are still in place at many of these companies.

We are all one or two great ideas away from more business opportunities than we can fully imagine. The marketing strategies roadmap in this book - when implemented with focus, commitment and care - are guaranteed to make you more money with less effort. These are strategies that have helped businesses just like yours make hundreds of thousands of dollars, and beyond, into 7-figures - including for your competitors. And, if you are willing to put in the work to implement these strategies, you will find yourself freed up with systems in place to grow your business and give you more free time and balance in your life.

Because I know exactly what you are going through as you grow your business, inspire your team, and seek balance in your life, I have dedicated my life to serving business owners and senior leaders. I understand and have seen the overwhelming demand for marketing, measurable results, structure, and accountability. I've felt firsthand the need of small business leaders to surround themselves with someone that cares as much as they do about their business, who can provide a profitable third party perspective and support. Many business leaders find that it is very lonely at the top.

As you read this book and the principles to follow, remember that every business faces common challenges. It doesn't matter what industry you're in, nor the type of business you operate (I've been part of many).

What matters is that you grasp the heart of the principles, the underlying lessons and strategies, that can help grow any enterprise in any business category imaginable. And that you are willing to take action!

The best time to start is NOW. We've got the roadmap. Let's get moving!

Dedicated to your success,

Christine Perakis, Esq.

PS. If you would like to arrange a meeting to get a profitable third party perspective on your business, email us at christine@christineperakis.com

To learn how to avoid the 3 key mistakes all small business owners make, visit www.businessbreakthroughpro.com

1

Start at the Beginning - Define Your Target Market

What is a Target Market?

Many businesses can't answer the question: *Who is your target market?* They have often made the fatal assumption that *everyone* will want to purchase their product or service with the right marketing strategy. We had an expression in the movie business that, "if you make a movie for everyone, you've made a movie for no one." It's critical that you find your ideal clients, those who have been waiting for what you have to offer.

In fact, many small business owners are simply daunted by the idea of getting really clear about who their target is and how to define them. Knowing your products and services well enough to identify what problem you are solving, or what result you are creating and for whom, will take you some distance to understanding who you are in business to serve.

A target market is simply the group of customers or clients who will purchase a specific product or service. This group of people all have something in common, often age, gender, hobbies, or location and more.

Your target market, then, consists of the people who will buy your offering. This includes both existing and potential customers, all of whom are motivated to do one of three things:

- Fulfill a need
- Solve a problem
- Satisfy a desire

To build, maintain, and grow your business, you need to know who your customers are, what they do, what they like, and why they would buy your product or service. You need to know the conversation going on in their minds, what problem they want to solve, or what result they seek that they haven't yet found. Getting this wrong – or not taking the time to get it right – will cost you time, money, and potentially the success of your business.

The Importance of Knowing Your Target Market

Knowledge and understanding of your target market is the keystone in the arch of your business. Without it, your product or service positioning, pricing, marketing strategy, and eventually, your business could very quickly fall apart. You are in business for a purpose. You understood the need well enough to create your products or services. That inspiration is a starting point for you to begin to know who else thinks like you do – those who see the need for what you are offering.

If you don't intimately know your target market, you run the risk of making mistakes when it comes to establishing pricing, product mix, or service packages. Your marketing strategy will lack direction, and produce mediocre results at best. Even if your marketing message and unique selling proposition (USP) are clear, and your brochure is perfectly designed, it means nothing unless it arrives in the hands (or ears) of the right people.

Determining your target market takes time and careful diligence. While it often starts with a best guess, assumptions cannot be relied on and research and testing is required to confirm original ideas. Your target market is not always your ideal market.

Once you build an understanding of who your target market is, keep up with your market research. Having your finger on the pulse of their motivations and drivers – which naturally change – will help you to anticipate needs or wants and evolve your business to stay ahead of your competition.

Types of Markets

Consumer

The Consumer Market includes those general consumers who buy products and services for personal use, or for use by family and friends. This is the market category you or I fall into when we're shopping for groceries or clothes, seeing a movie in the theatre, or going out for lunch. Retailers focus on this market category when marketing their goods or services.

Institutional

The Institutional Market serves society and provides products or services for the benefit of society. This includes hospitals, non-profit organizations, government organizations, schools and universities. Members of the Institutional Market purchase products to use in the provision of services to people in their care.

Business to Business (B2B)

The B2B Market is just what it seems to be: businesses that purchase the products and services of other business to run their operations. These purchases can include products that are used to manufacture other products (raw or technical), products that are needed for daily operations (such as office supplies), or services (such as accounting, shredding, and legal).

Reseller

This market can also be called the "Intermediary Market" because it consists of businesses that act as channels for goods and services between other markets. Goods are purchased and sold for a profit – without any alterations. Members of this market include wholesalers, retailers, resellers, and distributors.

Determining Your Target Market

Product / Service Investigation

The process for determining your target market starts by examining exactly what your offering is, and what the average customer's motivation for purchasing it is. Start by answering the following questions:

Does your offering meet a basic need?	
Does your offering serve a particular want?	
Does your offering fulfill a desire?	
What is the lifecycle of your product / service?	
What is the availability of your offering?	
What is the cost of the average customer's purchase?	
What is the lifecycle of your offering?	
How many times or how often will customers purchase your offering?	
Do you foresee any upcoming changes in your industry or region that may affect the sale of your offering (positive/negative)?	

Market Investigation

- **On the ground.** Spend some time on the ground researching who your target market might be. If you're thinking about opening a coffee shop, hang out in the neighborhood at different times of the day to get a sense of the people who live, work, and play in the neighborhood. Notice their age, gender, clothing, and any other indications of income and activities.

- **At the competition.** Who is your direct competitor targeting? Is there a small niche that is being missed? Observing the clientele of your competition can help to build understanding of your target market, regardless of whether it is the same or opposite. For example, if you own a children's clothing boutique and the majority of middle-class mothers shop at the local department store, you may wish to focus on higher-income families as your target market.

- **Online.** Many cities and towns – or at least regions – have demographic information available online. Research the ages, incomes, occupations, and other key pieces of information about the people who live in the area you operate your business. From this data, you will gain an understanding of the size of your total potential market.

- **With existing customers.** Talk to your existing customers through focus groups or surveys. This is a great way to gather demographic and behavioral information, as well as genuine feedback about product or service quality and other information that will be useful in a business or marketing strategy.

Who is Your Market?

Based on your product / service and market investigations, you will be able to piece together a basic picture of your target market, and some of their general characteristics. Record some notes here. At this point, you may wish to be as specific as possible, or maintain some generalities. You can further segment your market in the next section.

Consumer Target Market Framework

Market Type:	Consumer	
Gender:	☐ Male	☐ Female
Age Range:		
Purchase Motivation:	☐ Meet a Need ☐ Serve a Want ☐ Fulfill a Desire	
Activities:		
Income Range:		
Marital Status:		
Location:	☐ Neighborhood ☐ City ☐ Region ☐ Country	
Other Notes:		

Institutional Target Market Framework

Market Type:	Institutional
Institution Type:	☐ Hospital ☐ Non-profit ☐ School ☐ University ☐ Charity ☐ Government ☐ Church
Purchase Motivation:	☐ Operational Need ☐ Client Want ☐ Client Desire
Purpose of Institution:	
Institution's Client Base:	
Size:	
Location:	☐ Neighborhood ☐ City ☐ Region ☐ Country
Other Notes:	

B2B Target Market Framework

Market Type:	Business to Business (B2B)
Company Size:	
Number of Employees:	
Purchase Motivation:	☐ Operations Need ☐ Strategy ☐ Functionality
Annual Revenue:	
Industry:	
Location(s):	
Purpose of Business:	
People, Culture & Values:	
Other Notes:	

Reseller Target Market Framework

Market Type:	Reseller
Industry:	
Client Base:	
Purchase Motivation:	☐ Operations Need ☐ Client Wants ☐ Functionality
Annual Revenue:	
Age:	
Location:	☐Neighborhood☐ City ☐ Region ☐ Country
Other Notes:	

Your Target Market: Putting It Together

Based on the information you gather from your product / service and market study you should have a clear vision of your realistic target market. Here are a few examples of how this information is put together and conclusions are drawn:

Target Market Sample 1: Consumer Market

Business: Baby Clothing Boutique **Market Type:** Consumer **Gender:** Women **Marital Status:** Married	**Business Purpose:** *Meet a need* (provide clothing for infants and children aged 0 to 5 years) *Serve a want* (clothing is brand name only, and has a higher price point than the competition)
Market Observations: located on Main Street of Anytown, a street that is seeing many new boutiques open up, proximate to the main shopping mall two blocks from popular mid-range restaurant that is busy at lunch	**Industry Predictions:** large number of new housing developments in the city and surrounding areas two new schools in construction expect to see an influx of new families move to town from Anycity
Competition Observations: baby clothing also available at two local department stores, and one second-hand shop on opposite side of town	**Online Research:** half of Anytown's population is female, and 25% have children under the age of 15 years Anytown's population is expected to increase by 32% within three years The average household income for Anytown is $75,000 annually
TARGET MARKET: The target market can then be described as married mothers with children under five years old, between the ages of 25 and 45, who have recently moved to Anytown from Anycity, and have a household income of at least $100K annually.	

Target Market Sample 2: B2B Market

Business: Confidential Paper Shredding	**Target Business Size:** Small to medium
Market Type: B2B (Business to Business)	**Target Business Revenue:** $500K to $1M
Business Purpose: *Meet an operations need* (provide confidential on-site shredding services for business documents)	**Target Business Type:** produce or handle a variety of sensitive paper documentation accountants, lawyers, real estate agents, etc.
Market Observations: there are two main areas of office buildings and industrial warehouses in Anycity three more office towers are being constructed, and will be completed this year	**Industry Predictions:** the professional sector is seeing revenue growth of 24% over last year, which indicates increased client billing and staff recruitment
Competition Observations: one confidential shredding company serves the region, covering Anycity and the surrounding towns provide regular (weekly or biweekly) service, but does not have the capacity to handle large volumes at one time	**Online Research:** Anycity's biggest employment sectors are: manufacturing, tourism, food services, and professional services

TARGET MARKET:

The target market can then be described as small to medium sized businesses in the professional sector with an annual revenue of $500K to $1M who require both regular and infrequent large volume paper shredding services.

Segmenting Your Market

Your market segments are the groups within your target market – broken down by a determinant in one of the following four categories:

- Demographics
- Psychographics
- Geographics
- Behaviors

Segmenting your target market into several more specific groups allows you to further tailor your marketing campaign and more specifically position your product or service. You may wish to divide your ad campaign into four sections, and target four specific markets with messages that will most resonate with the audience.

For example, the baby clothing store may choose to segment its target market by psychographics, or lifestyle. If the larger target market is *married females with children under five, between the ages of 25 and 45, who have a household income of at least $100K annually*, it can be broken down into the following lifestyle segments:

- Fitness-oriented mothers
- Career-oriented mothers
- New mothers

With these three categories, unique marketing messages can be created that speak to the hot-buttons of each segment. The more accurate and specific you can make communications with your target market, the greater impact you will have on your revenues.

Market Segmentation Variables

Demographic	Psychographic	Geographic	Behavioristic
Age	Personality	Region	Brand Loyalty
Income	Lifestyle	Country	Product Usage
Gender	Values	City	Purchase
Generation	Attitude	Area	Frequency
Nationality	Motivation	Neighborhood	Profitability
Ethnicity	Activities	Density	Readiness to Buy
Marital Status	Interests	Climate	User Status
Family Size			
Occupation			
Religion			
Language			
Education			
Employment Type			
Housing Type			
Housing Ownership			
Political Affiliation			

Understanding Your Target Market

Once you have determined who your market is, make a point of learning everything you can about them. You need to have a strong understanding of who they are, what they like, where they shop, why they buy, and how they spend their time. Remind yourself that you may *think* you know your market, but until you have verified the information, you'll be driving your marketing strategy blind.

Also, be aware that markets change, just like people. Just because you knew your market when you started your business 10 years ago, doesn't mean you know it now. Regular market research is part of any successful business plan, and a great habit to start.

Having served the entertainment industry throughout my career, I had a birds' eye view of how essential it can be and what valuable information can be learned that makes a huge difference in the success of any business. In the world of entertainment, a movie studio is basically launching a new business every time a new movie is released, and there is no substitute for reliable market research when so many millions of dollars are at stake. And, for small business owners, the losses from not reaching your target market, even with fewer zeros, can hit even harder.

Types of Market Research

Surveys

The simplest way to gather information from your clients or target market is through a survey. You can craft a questionnaire full of questions about your product, service, market demographics, buyer motivations, and so on. Plus, anonymous surveys will produce the most accurate information since names are not attached to the results or specific comments.

Depending on the purpose—whether it is to gather demographic information, product or service feedback, or other data—there are a number of ways to administer a survey.

1. Telephone

Telephone surveys are a more time-consuming option, but have the benefit of live communication with your target market. Generally, it is best to have a third party conduct this type of survey to gather the most honest feedback. This is the method that market researchers use for polling, which is highly reliable, the 2016 election notwithstanding!

2. Online

Online surveys are the easiest to administer yourself. There are many web-based services that quickly and easily allow you to custom create your survey, and send it to your email marketing list. These services can also analyze, summarize and interpret the results on your behalf. Keep in mind that the results include only those who are motivated to respond, which may slant your results.

3. *Paper-based.*

Paper surveys are seldom used, and can prove to be an inefficient method. Like online surveys, your results are based on the feedback of those who were motivated for one reason or another to respond. However, the time and effort involved in taking the survey, filing it out, and returning it to your place of business may deter people from participating. If your business involves gathering your potential target market in any manner, you can use that opportunity to offer and receive completed handwritten surveys.

Keep in mind that surveys can be complex to administer, and consume more time and resources than you have planned. If you have the budget, consider hiring a professional market research firm to lead or assist with the process. This will also ensure that the methodology is standard practice, and will garner the most accurate results.

Website Analysis

Tracking your website traffic is an excellent way to research your existing and potential customer's interests and behavior. From this information, you can ensure the design, structure and content of your website is catering to the people who use it – and the people you want to use it.

User-friendly website traffic analytics programs can easily show you who is visiting your site, where they are from, and what pages of your site they are viewing. Services like Google Analytics can tell you what page they arrive at, where they click to, how much time they spend on each page, and on which page they leave the site.

This is powerful (and free!) information to have in your market research, and easy to monitor monthly or weekly, depending on the needs of your business.

Customer Purchase Data (Consumer Behavior)

If you do not have the budget to conduct your own professional market research, you can and should use existing resources on consumer behavior. While this data may not be specific to your region or city, general consumer research is actual data that can be helpful in confirming assumptions you may have made about your target market.

Your customer loyalty program or Point of Sale system may also be of help in tracking customer purchases and identifying trends in purchase behavior. If you can track who is buying, what they're buying and how often they're buying, you'll have an arsenal of powerful insight into your existing client base.

Focus Groups

Focus groups look at the psychographic and behavioristic aspects of your target market. Groups of six to 12 people are gathered and asked general and specific questions about their purchase motivations and behaviors. These questions could relate to your business in particular or to the general industry.

Focus group sessions can also be expensive and time consuming to organize and facilitate, so consider hiring the services of a professional market research firm. You may also receive more honest information if a third party is asking the questions, and receiving the responses from focus group participants.

For cost savings, consider partnering with an associate in the same industry who is not a direct competitor, and who would benefit from the same market data.

It is important to remember in utilizing any form of survey or research, that you are getting only a snapshot of that particular audience's point of view, and that may not tell the whole story. It is prudent to test any changes that you make, and not stop with any one survey. If you continue to test, even after you have created new content in response to any one survey, you will hone your message to be most accessible to your broadest target market.

2

Create Marketing Material with Your Target in Mind

Your marketing collateral has one purpose in the world: to act as an ambassador for your product or service, in place of *you*. This may seem like a big job for a piece of paper or a few screens, but it's a helpful way to think about the materials you create. In any business that I have been involved in, I always wanted to create my "swoosh" – the one symbol that exemplified my business, as Nike so successfully did for its business. Yet, I also had to ask, what would that symbol communicate to my target market about the benefits and value of buying from me?

When you meet with a potential or existing client, you do a number of things. You make sure you are well prepared with all the information the customer could need. You dress in clothing that is appropriate. You anticipate their needs, and offer a solution to their problems. You may also cater to how best they like to receive information, including identifying communication styles that will be most well-received. Talking about behavioral assessments is beyond the scope of this book, but needless to say, becoming adept at identifying and mirroring communication styles with your target market will serve you well.

Chances are, you wouldn't meet with clients just for the sake of meeting with a client – say, for instance, to show off your new suit. Likewise, you shouldn't create and distribute collateral that is non-essential.

We all know that the biggest challenge for small businesses is the limited number of zeros attached to their marketing budget. Marketing materials can be expensive, and a single, well-produced piece has the ability to devour the entire budget. Given that billion-dollar marketing campaigns fail every day, how can you be sure to make the most of, and be successful with, the dollars you're working within?

The answer? Limit yourself to only the essential items for your individual business, and produce them *well* with the resources you have.

Your Essential Marketing Materials

The easiest way to throw away your marketing budget is to create and produce marketing materials *you don't need*. Since many pieces of collateral are paper-based, this not only leaves you with boxes of extra (outdated) materials, but also takes a huge toll on the environment.

Take some time to determine what marketing materials you do need, and stick to your list. It's easy to want to "keep up with the Joneses" when your competition comes out with a new piece, but remember your focus should be on attracting and retaining a customer base, not matching the competition item for item.

Know your target market. Make sure you have a solid understanding of your customer base. From that knowledge, you can easily determine what the best way is to reach out and communicate with them. Are they a paper-based or techno savvy client group? Do they appreciate being contacted by email or mail? Are they impressed by flashy design, or simple pieces? *How* you communicate is often just as or more important than *what* you communicate.

Pay attention to costs. Do you really need a die-cut business card? Does your flyer absolutely require ink to the edges? Unique touches to marketing collateral can grab a customer's attention, but they can also dramatically increase the cost of production. Keep an eye out during the design process and make strategic choices about graphic elements.

Make mistakes – in small batches. Not sure if that flyer is going to do the trick? Testing out a limited time offer? Small production runs may cost a little more, but you'll avoid collecting boxes of unusable materials. Or, try a split run with different types or versions of the same piece and see what works best.

Keep the environment in mind. Environmental responsibility is on everyone's mind these days – including your customers. Always question if a particular marketing item can be produced in electronic format. Consider eliminating plastic bags in exchange for cloth ones, printed with your logo; print everything double-sided; send electronic newsletters; use your website to communicate; and, use recycled paper and envelopes when you can.

Brainstorm your wish list. Create a list of desired marketing materials, and ignore expenses, clients, or any other constraint. Then, beside each item, indicate realistically if it is a needed, wanted, not needed, or electronic item. The next page includes a checklist to get you started. Once you have finished, re-write your list in priority order. This will keep you focused on the essentials only.

Marketing Materials Checklist

Item	Need	Want	Don't Need	Electronic
Logo				
Business Cards				
Brochure				
Website				
Newsletter				
Catalogue				
Advertisements				
Flyers				
Fridge Magnet				
Branded Swag (pens, etc.)				
Employee Clothing				
Product Labels				
Signage				
Internal Templates (Fax Cover, Memo, etc.)				
Email Signature				
Blog				
Letterhead + Envelopes				
Thank You Cards				
Notepads				
Seasonal Gifts				
Company Profile				

Headlines + Sub headlines

If your headlines were all that a potential customer read, how do you think your marketing materials would fare? Headlines need to be bold, dramatic, shocking and absolutely answer the questions "What's in it for me?" or, "Why should I care?"

Headlines (and sub headlines) are vital in today's market because we are bombarded with so much information that we scan everything. Readers are skimming your materials to find out why they should bother paying attention to your product or service. Hit their hot buttons, and tell them why they should care, in your headlines!

Remember that headlines and sub headlines are not just for advertisements. They work wonders in newsletters, sales letters, brochures and websites, and can be incorporated into all of your essential marketing materials.

Design

The cost of professional design can eat up the majority of your marketing budget in a hurry. However, the cost of distributing materials that look and feel unprofessional can often be much higher. The key is to find the middle ground.

Unless you have design or desktop publishing experience – or even if you do – your time is probably not best spent designing your own marketing materials. Depending on the size of your business and your graphic needs (i.e., Do you need frequent photography of your products?) there are a number of options you can choose from:

1. **Hire a design agency.** This is no doubt the most costly of your options. However, if you have a number of items to be designed, you may be able to get a package rate. Another option is to have the design agency create a logo and stationery package for you, then create a "how-to" style guide for use of the logo, fonts, and other graphic elements in the rest of your marketing materials. My last business had a style guide created by our designer that was very useful as a reference, particularly as the business expanded into new product lines.

2. **Hire a freelance designer.** For most small businesses, the benefits of using a freelance designer (aside from cost savings) are convenience and trust. If you are lucky enough to find one you work well with, work hard to establish a seamless working relationship and you'll never worry about the design of your marketing materials again. Ask colleagues for recommendations of local designers, or review any number of professional sites that offer freelance services sites at very reasonable costs. You can often find everything you need and will be able to review their work to see if it aligns with your sensibilities. I have found that having a good relationship with a designer is essential to maintaining consistency of message, look and feel throughout the life of the business.

3. **Hire a part-time design employee.** Need to hire someone part-time for a task around the office or shop? Consider recruiting someone with design skills and hiring them for full-time work. This could

include graphic design students, or someone with an interest (and talent) in the field.

4. **Hire an Intern.** Go to the local college in your area and engage a design student as an intern to work with you in your business. It can be very cost effective, cutting edge and hugely rewarding for all involved.

Whichever option you choose – or if you choose to design your materials yourself - the two most important things to remember about design are:

1. **Keep it consistent.** Your marketing materials must be consistent, or your customers will never learn to recognize your brand.

2. **Keep it simple.** Simple, clean design is the most effective way of communicating. Use "wow" pieces sparingly.

Guidelines for the Top 10 Marketing Materials

Logo

- **Use design resources.** If you are going to spend any money on outside design help, this is the time to do it. Your logo is the visual representation of your product or service, and appears on everything that relates to your business. This is the core of your brand image, and needs to be done right the first time.

- **Remember the purpose.** The logo needs to be a unique reflection of your business, your business values, and the industry you work in. Before you commit to your logo, make sure to give careful consideration to color choice, image selection and image recognition – as well as the logos that already exist in the marketplace. Test it out on your family and friends for an outside opinion and use their feedback.

- **Don't get too complicated.** Can it be produced (and seen clearly) in black and white? In a single color? With your company name? Too often businesses design their own logos that include a complex assortment of photos, words, and solid design elements. These do not photocopy well, and can't be clearly read at a small scale. Keep your logo design down to a graphic image and the name of your business. And, remember that it should stand out if printed in black and white, or viewed on a small mobile screen.

Business cards

- **Cover the basics**. A business card needs to communicate your basic contact information to potential clients, including who you are and *what your business does*. Make sure you've covered the basics and made it easy for them to be in touch.

   o **Name**
   o **Title**
   o **Company Name**
   o **Company Slogan / Description**

- Phone Number
- Email Address
- Fax Number
- Address
- Cell Number (if applicable)
- Website

- **Make it memorable. Be creative.** Choose interesting shapes, die-cuts, orientation (vertical vs. horizontal), bright colors, and unique materials (wood, plastic, magnet, aluminum or foam). You don't have to go crazy or spend lots of money to do this – simple, clever twists on basic design make an impact. Just keep it relevant to your product or service. Don't be afraid to use your Headline and Subheader that tells your target exactly how you're going to solve a problem that they have and don't want, or create a result that they want and don't have.

- **Give them a reason to keep it.** What is going to keep them from throwing it out, or filing it in a 3" binder of other cards? Make the card worth keeping by adding something useful to the backside. For example, coffee shops put frequent buyer incentives on the backside of their cards, encouraging customers to keep them in their wallets. Other examples include pick-up schedules, reminders, calendars, testimonials, or coupons.

- **Produce a high quality card.** Use at least 100lb card stock, and print in color. Choose clear, easy to read fonts that aren't any smaller than 9pt.

Letterhead

- **Ensure a professional quality.** Letterhead that is simple, clean, and well produced allows the reader to focus on the important part: the content. Have your letterhead professionally printed on 32lb paper, or choose a textured stock. Show that you are invested in the professionalism of your company.

- **Pay attention to design choices.** The design of your marketing collateral should reflect your corporate values and the personality of your organization. If you are environmentally conscious, choose recycled paper and write it in small print at the bottom of the page. Letterhead can also be a place for subtle graphic elements, like watermarks, in addition to your logo.

- **Keep consistent with other materials.** Your letterhead is part of your stationery package, and should look and feel the same as the rest of your pieces. For example, if your business cards have been printed with rounded corners, so should your letterhead. Use consistent fonts, colors, and logo placement on your letterhead, business cards, fax cover sheets, and other internal documents to ensure recognition and ease of readability. There have been instances, too, where I have never needed print letterhead to run a business. So many people are getting accustomed to electronic communications that it may not be a necessary investment if your budget limits you.

Brochures

- **Cover the basics.** Each brochure you produce should include your basic marketing message, USP, and detailed company contact information. Product or service features, and customer benefits should be clearly displayed and described.

- **Be purpose-focused.** Why are you producing this brochure? Are you featuring a new product line? Trying to increase awareness? Introducing your service to a new market? Stay closely connected to the purpose behind your brochure, and ensure that all of the information (and images) in the brochure support that purpose.

- **Keep it simple.** Make sure the design and information organization is clean and easy to navigate. Like advertisements, leaving blank spaces gives the reader a break and makes it easier to narrow in on key messages.

- **Choose high quality production.** If you don't invest in your business, why should anyone else? Produce your brochure on high quality paper, in vivid color, and have it professionally folded. An impressive-looking brochure will travel farther than a homemade one – from one client's hands to another's.

- **Keep it fresh.** If you produce brochures on a regular basis, consider giving each a theme to distinguish the information as new and interesting. Keep the overall look and feel consistent, but play with images and content layout to revitalize the design. And don't forget to have fun with it. I remember my very first brochure and how much I enjoyed putting the content together and how proud I continued to be whenever I handed it out, for years after I originally created it. The best material is that content that you can look back on later and recognize that the messages are still relevant and true for your business.

Newsletters

- **Be in touch.** Don't wait until your existing clients walk back into your store. Show them they're important to your business, and keep them updated on new products and services by consistently distributing a personalized well-designed newsletter. The more personal you are willing to be, the more likely you will make an impact with your audience. Don't be afraid to be vulnerable when sharing stories from which you have learned and benefitted in ways that you may also help your clients do the same.

- **Use an online distribution service.** Online email marketing tools (CRM tools) have never been easier or cheaper to use, and enable you to personalize your letters without much effort. They will also track for you which clients open their newsletters, and which click through to your website. This information is invaluable market research data and should not be overlooked.

- **Provide information, tell a story.** Engage the reader with a short anecdote, or a piece of relevant information. Many people are bombarded by hard-copy and electronic letters on a daily basis, so make sure yours is worthy of their reading time. Include an "experts corner" or "new product feature" and structure the newsletter like your own business newspaper. Add links to relevant media articles, or special offers.

- **Choose a frequency you can maintain.** Newsletters can be time consuming, so be realistic about how often you promise to distribute them. This depends on your resources, and the needs of your business, but generally once a month to once every three months is a good time frame.

Company (or Corporate) Profile

- **Your ultimate company brochure.** Your company profile includes all pertinent information on your business and your offering, and acts as the base for all other marketing items. These are generally longer pieces – from five to 20 pages in length, allowing you ample room for written and visual content.

- **Tell your story.** The company profile is the place to tell the story of your business. Engage the reader, use anecdotes, and describe how and why your company was created. If you inherited the family business, describe how you're carrying on tradition and instilling new life. If you created your company from scratch with your college roommate, let the reader know. These real life details are interesting and establish trust with your potential clients and associates.

- **Communicate your values.** Here you have the space to describe your company's vision, values and approach, or philosophies. Make sure you relate your values to your offering, and keep this section short and succinct.

- **Explain your offering – features, benefits and all.** Just like your brochure, make sure to describe the full benefits and features of your product or service. Sprinkle testimonials throughout the design to back up your statements. This can include your full range of services, or simply an overview of your product types. Use professional images and creative copy to keep readers engaged.

- **Choose high-quality design and production.** Spend time creating a company profile that will last. Then, spend money producing one that will impress. Choose glossy paper, and a high-quality press, and leave the profiles around your store and office for clients to read and admire.

Signage

- **Get professional advice.** Outdoor signage can be a daunting task for anyone who hasn't designed, produced, or otherwise gone through the process. Since signage is influenced by a variety of factors – one of which is your municipal government signage bylaw – you may wish to enlist the help of a professional (a signage designer or printer) to guide you through the process and avoid costly errors.

- **Make it visible.** All of your outdoor signage should be easily seen from the street, or within the plaza or complex you are located in. In some cases, you may need more than one sign to do this. Keep in mind how your sign will look at night, as well as during the day, as your company logo and phone number or website needs to be visible at all times. For one of my businesses, we created a 22-foot freeway-frontage sign in vivid and visible color that was one of our most effective marketing pieces. Prior to making this invaluable investment, we drove up and down freeways, looking at the most attractive and easily spotted signs in use.

- **Make it distinct.** When it comes to signage, you can get really creative with materials, lights, and colors. While you need to maintain logo, color, and font consistency, you can add other graphic elements that may not work on the rest of your collateral, including 3D elements and window treatments. Make it memorable.

- **Remember your indoor signage.** Every business needs indoor signage to continually remind customers where they are. This includes section signage, product signage, way finding systems, and promotion announcements. If your business is located in an office, consider signage with your logo and company name above the reception area. Again, keep this signage consistent with the rest of your company materials, and you will be contributing to brand recognition.

Advertisements + Flyers

- **Place ads strategically.** Once you have determined who your target market is, you need to focus on advertising in the publications they are most likely to read, and distributing flyers in places they are most likely to be. Spend ad dollars strategically, and don't spend them all at once. Take time to test what publications work, and which don't, by measuring the response from each placement. And, when you place ads, request placement that is well-forward and in the top right hand corner.

- **Grab their attention.** You have less than half a second to grab the attention of your audience with print advertising, so use it wisely. Spend the bulk of your time crafting the headline and choosing compelling images.

- Make sure that any photography is done professionally and do not skimp on this. In one of my businesses, we created a product to protect professional racing drivers from rib injuries, and I remember how difficult it was to photograph for the original launch campaign. I worked hard with our photographer to get it just right. If we had tried to do it without the professional, we would have never been as effective. The mailing campaign that we did made our launch extremely successful, securing national distribution of our product line from the professional materials we created.

- **Keep their attention.** If you caught their attention, you have another two seconds to keep it. Use subheadings to further entice them to read on for the details of your product or service offer.

- **Tell them why they should buy.** Always include your marketing message or USP in your advertising. Describe the benefits and features of your product or service, but focus on the benefits that will trigger an emotional response from your target audience – love, money, luxury, convenience, and security, among others.

- **Tell them how they can buy.** Include a call to action beside your contact information, and include your phone number, website address, and business address (if applicable). You may wish to include a scarcity or urgency offer to compel your readers to act fast.

41

- **Know the importance of white space.** If you try to cram too much information into your ad or flyer, your readers will skip it. Clean, clear, easy to read ads and one-page flyers with succinct messages are most effective.

Website

- **Be purpose-focused.** Like your brochure, your website can serve a number of purposes. To be effective, you need to narrow in on the specific purpose when designing the content structure of the pages. Who is your audience? What do you want them to leave the site knowing? What do you want the site to make them do? Visit your store? Buy your offering? Pick up the phone? Make sure you are clear on this point before you start.

- **Make the address easy to remember (and find!).** A website address that is too long or too complicated will not get remembered, or found. Do a search for available website addresses that relate to your business or marketing message, and try to secure a site with a .com ending. If your company name is taken, use your USP or guarantee instead.

- **Focus on content.** The overall structure of how you organize the content on your site is like the foundation of your house. You can change the paint color, and the furniture, but the foundation is more or less there for good. Before you work with a designer and create the visual fabric of your website, focus on creating solid copy that is clearly organized. Put together a map of your structure, starting with your homepage and subpages, and allocating specific content to each page.

- **Revitalize regularly.** Your company is always changing, and so should your website. This is an important (and relatively inexpensive) way to communicate your company news and achievements, and most likely the easiest accessed source of information. Have areas for easy content updates – like a "news" section – and make sure sections like "employees" and "services" are kept up to date. For larger updates, go back to your purpose and website map, and make sure the content changes still support the original intent of the website.

- **Organize for intuition.** Make key information easy to access – especially your contact information. You can quickly tell if a website is easy to navigate, because the information you are looking for appears in a natural order. For example, when visiting a restaurant website, a link to the reservations page is provided on the menu page. While you're putting together your website map, do some research online and investigate what does and doesn't work. A good rule of thumb is to ensure it takes no more than three clicks to access a page. Bury content too deep, and your audience will get frustrated and leave.

- **Keep consistent with marketing materials.** Your website is an extension of your marketing campaign, and should be treated as such. Use consistent logo placements, fonts, colors and images so that all elements of your collateral are unified and likewise with marketing campaigns. If you are running a new promotion, or featuring a new item in an advertisement, include that information on your website. Customers responding to the ad will be reinforced, and customers who did not see the ad will be aware of the offer.

- Make your content relevant to what your target is looking for. These days, key words, tags and search engine placement are critical to cutting through the noise and being seen by your target audience. Just as with a print piece, every page of your site should address your target's needs and desires completely and consistently.

- **Measure your results.** Your website is a piece of your marketing collateral, just like brochures and advertisements, and should be evaluated for effectiveness on a regular basis. Easy website analysis tools, like Google Analytics, will show you which pages your audience is viewing, how long they're staying on each page, and where and when they leave the site. That is powerful information when it comes to structuring content, and choosing on which page to put your most important messages.

3

Make an Offer Your Target Can't Refuse

I'm going to tell it to you straight:

Your offer is the cornerstone of your marketing campaign.

Get it right, and everything else will fall into place. Your headline will grab readers, your copy will sing, your ad layout will hardly matter, and you will have customers running to your door.

Get it wrong, and even the best looking, best-written campaign will sink like the Titanic.

A powerful offer is an irresistible offer. It's an offer that gets your audience frothing at the mouth and clamoring over each other all the way to your door. An offer that makes your readers pick up the phone and open their wallets.

Irresistible offers make your potential customers think, "I'd be crazy not to take him up on that," or "An offer like this doesn't come around very often." They instill a sense of emotion, of desire, and ultimately, urgency. Haven't you ever felt that way about something that you came across that felt irresistible, even if you weren't sure why?

Make it easy for customers to purchase from you the first time, and spend your time keeping them coming back.

I'll say it again: **get it right, and everything else will fall into place.**

The Crux of Your Marketing Campaign

As you work your way through this program, you will find that nearly every chapter discusses the importance of a powerful offer as related to your marketing strategy or promotional campaign.

There's a reason for this. The powerful offer is more often than not the reason a customer will open their wallets. It is how you generate leads, and then convert them into loyal customers. The more dramatic, unbelievable, and valuable the offer is the more dramatic and unbelievable the response will be.

Many companies spend thousands of dollars on impressive marketing campaigns in glossy magazines and big city newspapers. They send massive direct mail campaigns on a regular basis; yet don't receive an impressive or massive response rate.

These companies do not yet understand that simply providing information on their company and the benefits of their product is not enough to get customers to act. There is no reason to pick up the phone or visit the store, *right now*.

Your powerful, irresistible offer can:

- Increase leads
- Drive traffic to your website or business
- Move old product
- Convert leads into customers
- Build your customer database

What Makes an Irresistible Offer?

An irresistible offer is one that makes the most people respond, and take action. It gets people running to spend money on your product or service.

Powerful offers nearly always have an element of *urgency* and of *scarcity*. They give your audience a reason to act immediately, instead of putting it off until a later date.

Urgency relates to time. The offer is only available until a certain date, during a certain period of the day, or if you act within a few hours of seeing the ad. The customer needs to act now to take advantage of the offer.

Scarcity related to quantity. There are only a certain number of customers who will be able to take advantage of the offer. There may be a limited number of spaces, a limited number of products, or simply a limited number of people the business will provide the offer to. Again, this requires that customer acts immediately to reap the high value for low cost.

Powerful, irresistible offers also:

Offer great value. Customers perceive the offer as having great value – more than a single product on its own, or the product at its regular price. It is clear that the offer takes the reader's needs and wants into consideration.

Make sense to the reader. They are simple and easy to understand if read quickly. Avoid percentages – use half off or 2 for 1 instead of 50% off. There are no "catches" or requirements; no fine print.

Seem logical. The offer doesn't come out of thin air. There is a logical reason behind it – a holiday, end of season, anniversary celebration, or new product. People can get suspicious of offers that seem "too good to be true" and have no apparent purpose.

Provide a premium. The offer provides something extra to the customer, like a gift, or free product or service. They feel they are getting something extra for no extra cost. Premiums are perceived to have more value than discounts.

Remember that when your target market reads your offer, they will be asking the following questions:

1. What are you offering me?
2. What's in it for me?

3. What makes me sure I can believe you?

4. How much do I have to pay for it?

The Most Powerful Types of Offers

Decide what kind of offer will most effectively achieve your objectives. Are you trying to generate leads, convert customers, build a database, move old product off the shelves, or increase sales?

Consider what type of offer will be of most value to your ideal customers – what offer will make them act quickly.

Free Offer

This type of offer asks customers to act immediately in exchange for something free. This is a good strategy to use to build a customer database or mailing list. Offer a free consultation, free consumer report, or other item of low cost to you but of high perceived value.

You can also advertise the value of the item you are offering for free. For example, act now and you'll receive a free consultation, worth $75 dollars. This will dramatically increase your lead generation, and allow you to focus on conversion when the customer comes through the door or picks up the phone.

The Value Added Offer

Add additional services or products that cost you very little, and combine them with other items to increase their attractiveness. This increases the perception of value in the customer's mind, which will justify increasing the price of a product or service without incurring extra hard costs to your business.

For example, as we discuss below, if you know of a complimentary product that your customers are looking for or would want, and you can procure these at a lower cost than they would, you can offer something of high value, even if you increase your own prices.

Package Offer

Package your products or services together in a logical way to increase the perceived value, as a whole. Discount the value of the package by a small margin, and position it as a "start-up kit" or "special package." By packaging goods of mixed values, you will be able to close more high-value sales. For example: including a free desk-jet printer with every computer purchase.

Premium Offer

Offer a bonus product or service with the purchase of another. This strategy will serve your bottom line much better than discounting. This includes 2 for 1 offers, offers that include free gifts, and in-store credit with purchases over a specific dollar amount.

Urgency Offer

As I mentioned above, offers that include an element of urgency enjoy a better response rate, as there is a reason for your customers to act immediately. Give the offer a deadline or limit the number of spots available.

Guarantee Offer

Offer to take the risk of making a purchase away from your customers. Guarantee the performance or results of your product or service, and offer to compensate the customer with their money back if they are not satisfied. This will help overcome any fear or reservations about your product, and make it more likely for your leads to become customers.

Create Your Powerful Offer

1. Pick a single product or service.

Focus on only one product or service – or one product or service *type* – at a time. This will keep your offer clear, simple, and easy to understand. This can be an area of your business you wish to grow, or old product that you need to move off the shelves.

2. Decide what you want your customers to do.

What are you looking to achieve from your offer? If it is to generate more leads, then you'll need your customer to contact you. If it is to quickly sell old product, you'll need your customer to come into the store and buy it. Do you want them to visit your website? Sign up for your newsletter? How long do they have to act? Be clear about your call to action, and state it clearly in your offer.

3. Dream up the biggest, best offer.

First, think of the biggest, best things you could offer your customers – regardless of cost and ability. Don't limit yourself to a single type of offer, combine several types of offers to increase value. Offer a premium, plus a guarantee, with a package offer. Then, take a look at what you've created, and make the necessary changes so it is realistic.

4. Run the numbers.

Finally, make sure the offer will leave you with some profit – or at least allow you to break even. You don't want to publish an outrageous offer that will generate a tremendous number of leads, but leave you broke. Remember that each customer has an acquisition cost, as well as a lifetime value. The amount of their first purchase may allow you to break even, but the amount of their subsequent purchases may make you a lovely profit.

4

We're All in Sales

If you're a business owner, you're also a salesperson.

You've had to sell the bank to get them to loan you your start-up capital. You've had to sell the best employees on why they should work for your business. You've had to convince your business partner, spouse, and maybe even your friends and family why your business idea is a good one.

Now you have to repeatedly sell your product or service to your customers.

The ability to sell effectively and efficiently is one every successful business owner has cultivated, and continues to develop. It can be a complicated and time consuming task, one that you will have to continually work on throughout your career in order to be – and stay – successful.

Fortunately, making sales is a step-by-step process that can be learned, customized, and continuously improved. There are a wide range of tools available to help and support your sales efforts.

You don't have to be the most outgoing, enthusiastic person to be successful at sales. You don't even have to be a good public speaker. All you need is an understanding of the basic sales process, the target market and their needs, and a genuine passion for what you are selling, knowing that it fulfills the needs of your target market.

Sales 101

As I said before, making sales is a process. There are clear, step-by-step actions that can be taken and result in a sale.

The sales process varies according to the type of business, type of customers and type of product or service that is offered; however, the core steps are the same. Similarly, sales training varies from individual to individual, but the core skills and abilities remain the same.

Here is a basic seven-step process that you can follow, or fine tune to suit your unique products and services. Remember that each step is important, and builds on the step previous. It is essential to become adept at each step, instead of solely focusing on closing the sale.

1. Preparation

Make sure you have prepared for your meeting, presentation, or day on the sales floor. You have complete control of this part of the sales process, so it is important to do everything you can to set the stage for your success.

- Understand your product or service inside and out.
- Be clear about what problem you believe you are solving, or what result you are going to achieve with your product or service for your target market
- Prepare all the necessary materials, and organize them neatly.
- Keep your place of business tidy and organized. Make sure product is visible and attractive on shelves.
- Ensure you appear professional and well groomed.
- Do some research on your potential client and brainstorm to find common ground between your potential client and you or your product and services.

2. Build a Relationship

The first few minutes you spend with a potential customer set the stage for the rest of your interaction. First impressions are everything. Your goal in the second step is to relax the customer and begin to develop a relationship with them. Establishing a real relationship with your customer will create trust.

- Make a great first impression: shake hands, make eye contact, and introduce yourself.
- Remain confident and professional, but also personable.
- Mirror their speech, style of communication and behavior.
- Begin with general questions and small talk.
- Show interest in them and their place of business.
- Notice and comment on positives.
- Find some common interests, needs and desires on which to relate.

3. Discuss Needs + Wants

Once you have spent a few moments getting to know your prospect, start asking open-ended questions to discover some of their needs and wants. If they have come to you on the sales floor, ask what brought them in the store. If you are meeting them to present your product or service, ask why they are interested, or what criteria they have in mind for that product or service.

- If you are making a sales presentation, ask for a few moments at the outset to outline the purpose of your visit, as well as how you have structured the presentation.
- Listen intently, and repeat back information you are not sure you understand.
- Ask open-ended questions to get them talking. The longer they talk, the more insight they are providing you into their needs and purchase motivations.
- Ask clarifying questions about their responses.
- If you become sure the customer is going to buy your product or service, begin to ask questions specific to the offering. i.e., what size/color do you prefer?

4. Present the Solution

Once you have a solid understanding of what they are looking for, or what issue they are looking to resolve, you can begin to present the solution: your product or service.

- Explain how your product or service will solve their problem or meet their needs. If several products apply, begin by presenting the mid-level product.
- Illustrate your points with anecdotes about other happy customers, or awards the product or service has earned.
- Use hypothetical examples featuring your customer. Encourage them to picture a scenario after their purchase.
- Always begin by describing the benefits of the product, then follow up with features and advantages.
- Watch your customer's behavior as you speak, and ask further qualifying questions in response to body language and verbal comments.
- Give the customer an opportunity to ask you questions or provide feedback about each product or service after you have described or explained it.
- Ask closed-ended questions to gain agreement.

5. Overcome Objections

As you present the product or service, take note of potential objections by asking open-ended questions and monitoring body language. Expect that objections will arise and prepare for it. Consider brainstorming a list of all potential objections, and writing down your responses.

- Repeat the objection back to the customer to ensure you understand them correctly.
- Empathize with what they have said, and then provide a response that overcomes the objection.
- Confirm that the answer you have provided has overcome their objection by repeating yourself.

The Eight Most Common Objections
The product or service does not seem valuable to me. There is no reason for me to act now. I will wait. It's safest not to make a decision right away. There is not enough money for the purchase. The competitor or another department offers a better product. There are internal issues between people or departments. The relationship with the decision maker is strained. There is an existing contract in place with another business.

6. Close

This is an important part of the sales process that should be handled delicately. Deciding when to close is a judgment call that must be made in the moment during the sale. Ideally, you have presented a solution to their problem, overcome objections, and have the customer in a place where they are ready to buy.

Here are some questions to ask before you close the sale:

- Does my prospect agree that there is value in my product or service?
- Does my prospect understand the benefits and features of the product or service?
- Are there any remaining objections that must be handled?
- What other factors could influence my prospect's decision to buy?
- Have I minimized the risk involved in the purchase, and provided some level of urgency?

Once you have determined it is time to make the sale, here are some sample statements you can use to get the process rolling:

- So, should we get started?
- Shall I grab a new one from the back?
- If you just give me your credit card, I can take care of the transaction while you continue browsing.
- When would you like the product delivered?
- We can begin next month if we receive payment by the end of the week.
- Can I email you a draft contract tomorrow?

7. Service + Follow-up

Once you have made the sale, your work is not over. You want to ensure that customer will become a loyal, repeat customer, and that they will refer their friends to your business.

Ask them to be in your customer database, and keep in touch with regular newsletters. Follow up with a phone call or drop by to ask how they are enjoying the product or service, and if they have any further questions or needs you can assist them with.

This contact opportunity will also allow you ask for a referral, or an upsell. At the very least, it will ensure you are continuing to foster and build a relationship with the client.

Upselling

Upselling is simply inviting your customers to spend more money in your business by purchasing additional products or services. This could include more of the same product, complementary products, or impulse items.

Regardless, upselling is an effective way to increase profits and create loyal clients – without spending any money to acquire the business. These clients are already purchasing from you – which means they perceive value in what you have to offer – so take the information you have gained in the sales process and offer them a little bit more.

You experience upselling on a daily basis. From "do you want fries with that?" to "have you heard about our product protection program?" Companies across the globe have tapped into and trained their staff on the value of the upsell.

Upselling is truly rooted in good customer service. If your client purchases a new computer printer, you'll need to make sure they have the right cables required to connect it to the computer, regular and photo paper, and color and black and white ink.

If you don't suggest these items, they may arrive home and realize they do not have all the materials needed to use the product. They may choose to purchase those materials somewhere closer, cheaper, or more helpful.

Customer education is another form of upselling. What if your customer doesn't realize that you sell a variety of printer paper and stationery in addition to computer hardware like printers? Take every opportunity to educate your customer on the products and services you offer that may be of interest to them.

An effective way of implementing an upsell system into your business is simply by creating add-on checklists for the products or services you offer. Each item has a list of related items that your customer may need. This will encourage your staff to develop the habit of asking for the upsell.

Other upsell strategies can be implemented:

- **At the point of sale**. This is a great place for impulse items and you see it at grocery stores checkout – candy, flashlights, nail scissors, etc.

- **In a newsletter**. This is an effective strategy for customer education.

- **In your merchandising**. Place strips of impulse items near related items. For example, paper clips with paper and pens near binders.

- **Over the phone**. If someone is placing an order for delivery, offer additional items in the same shipment for convenience.

- **With new products**. Feature each new product or service that you offer prominently in your business, and ask your staff to mention it to every customer.

Anyone who shops Amazon can see how well this is done on their product pages, showing customers related products, potential peripheral purchases, even popular competitive or related products, no matter what product you are reviewing to purchase. And if you are like the rest of us, once you've looked at any product on Amazon, you will get follow up emails offering similar, competitive, alternative items available well after you have discontinued your search!

Sales Team

Employing a team of strong salespeople will translate directly to your bottom line profits.

What Makes a Good Salesperson?

There are a lot of salespeople out there – but what qualities and skills make a great salesperson? These are the attributes you will want to find or develop in your team:

- Willingness to continuously learn and improve sales skills
- Sincerity in relating to customers and providing solutions to their objectives
- An understanding of the company's big picture
- A communication style that is direct, polite, and professional
- Honesty and respect for other team members, customers, as well as the competition.
- Ability to manage time
- Enthusiastic
- Inquisitive
- A great listener
- Ability to quickly interpret, analyze, and respond to information during the sales process
- Ability to connect and develop relationships of trust with potential clients
- Professional appearance

Team Building – Keeping Your Team Together

In many businesses, Sales is a department or a whole team of people who work together to generate leads and convert customers. Effective management of your sales team is a skill every business owner should cultivate.

Teambuilding, recruitment, and training will be discussed in later sections, but take some time to consider the following aspects of managing a sales team:

Communication
- Are targets and results regularly reviewed?
- Are opportunities for input regularly provided?
- Do sales staff members have a clear understanding of what is expected?
- Do all staff members know daily, weekly, and quarterly targets?

Performance Management
- Are sales staff members motivated to reach targets – is there an understanding of workplace motivators within the team?
- Are sales staff recognized and rewarded once those targets are reached?
- Are there opportunities for skills training and development?
- Do staff members have broad and comprehensive product or industry knowledge?
- Is there opportunity for growth within the company?

- Is performance regularly reviewed?
- Does the program offer financial or other incentives for professional growth that may motivate the team?

Operations
- Do you have a solid understanding of your sales numbers (revenue, profit, margins)?
- Are your sales processes regularly reviewed?
- Do you have a variety of sales scripts prepared?
- Do you measure conversion rates?
- How are your leads generated?

Sales Tools

Every salesperson should have an arsenal of tools on hand to assist them in the sales process. These tools can act as aids while a sale is taking place, or help to foster continual learning and development of the salesperson's skills and approach. If your business does not have this, then they should be prepared so that anyone who is performing these functions or may be hired in the future, will have exactly what they need to do the very best job they can.

The list below includes some popular sales tools. Add to this list other resources that are specific to your business or industry.

Tool	Description + Benefit
Scripts	Used for incoming and outgoing telemarketing, cold calls, door-to-door sales, in-store sales Create several different scripts throughout your business Maintains consistency in your sales approach Revise and renew your scripts regularly
Presentation Materials	High-quality information about your product or service Forms: PowerPoint presentation, brochure, product sheets, proposal Serves as an outline of your sales presentation, and keeps you on task
Colleagues	A source of help and advice, especially when you are on the same team or sell similar products Also a source of support
Customer Databases	An accurate, up-to-date database of customer contact information and contact history Used to stay in touch with clients Can also be used for direct mail and follow-up telemarketing
The Internet	A powerful resource for sales help and advice Information to help improve your sales process Online sales coaching Source for product knowledge
Ongoing Training	Constant improvement of your sales skills Constant increase in product knowledge Investment in yourself and your company

8 Tips for Better Sales

- **Dress for the sale.** Dress professionally, appear well put together and maintain good hygiene. Ensure you are not only dressed professionally, but *appropriately*. Would your client feel more comfortable if you wore a suit, or jeans and a blazer? Think about what you are selling and how your prospect might be expecting you to appear and dress. Coming from the entertainment industry as I do, the "dress code" is very different than in banking, which might, in turn be very different for an industrial enterprise, for example.

- **Speak their language.** Show you understand their industry or culture, and use phrases your customer understands. This may require researching industry jargon or common phrases. Remember to avoid using words and phrases that have historically been used in the sales process: sold, contract, telemarketing, finance, interest, etc. Doing so will help break down the salesperson/customer barrier. Also, in my work, we conduct and become versed at DISC communication styles – learning how to detect the four distinct communication styles, a combination of which are represented in everyone. With training, we then learn to mirror and match those that you are speaking with. Becoming adept at this technique can take you a long way in your business. Check out my website if you'd like to learn more about how knowledge and skill at using DISC can help you be more successful in your communications.

- **Ooze positivity.** Show up or answer the phone with a smile, and leave your personal or business issues behind. Be enthusiastic about what you have to offer, and how that offering will benefit your customer. Reflect this not only in your voice, but also in your body language. Remember that this should be sincere, so even if you have been having a bad day before the encounter, develop and use whatever techniques work for you to shift your energies so that you can be genuinely happy to see your prospect. Know that the schedule you created is purposeful and that your meeting can actually lift you up and out of whatever you may have left behind at the office.

- **Deliver a strong pitch or presentation.** Be confident and convincing. Leave self-doubt at the door, and walk in assuming the sale. If you're invited in, then your potential client is already interested in hearing what you have to say. Take time to explain complex concepts, and always connect what you're saying to your audience in a specific way.

- **Be a poster-child for good manners.** Accept any amenity you're offered, listen intently, don't interrupt, don't show up late, have a strong handshake, and give everyone you are speaking to equal attention.

- **Avoid sensitive subjects.** Politics, religion, swearing, sexual innuendos and racial comments are should be off-limits. So are negative comments about other customers or the competition.

- **Create a real relationship.** Icebreakers and small talk are not just to pass the time before your presentation. They are how relationships get established. Show genuine interest in everything your customer has to say. Ask questions about topics for which you know they are passionate. Speak person to person, not salesperson to customer. Remember everything. I used to have difficulty remembering people's names almost as soon as they had spoken them. I was often so embarrassed. I realized that I would need to work on this "flaw" and embrace the embarrassment, confronting it head on. As I was working to overcome this issue, I would let people know and admit to my embarrassment. We could then laugh about it and I would never forget the new person's name. I've become more adept at retaining the new name, but I always repeat it when I first hear it, "Joe, so nice to meet you!", to ingrain it in my brain. It can get really tricky when I'm in my Caribbean home, where although English is the primary language, there are many different dialects and accents.

- **Know more than you need to.** Impress clients with comprehensive knowledge – not only of your product or service – but also of the people who use that product or service, and industry trends. Let yourself be seen as an expert in order to build trust and respect.

5

Double your Referrals

What if I told you that you could put an inexpensive system in place that would effectively allow your business to grow itself?

For most business owners, a large part of their customer base is comprised of referral customers. These people found out about the company's products or services from the recommendation of a friend or colleague who had a positive experience purchasing from that company. For my part, I've made multiple careers almost entirely based on referrals.

If your business benefits from referral customers – and what business doesn't really, unless you're a billion-dollar brand like McDonald's or Coca-Cola? When you are contacted by a referral, you will find that these customers arrive ready to buy from you, and tend to buy more often. They also tend to be highly loyal to your product or service.

Seem like the best kind of customers to have, don't they?

Referral customers cost less to acquire. Compared to the leads you generate from advertising, direct mail campaigns, and other marketing initiatives, referral customers come to you already qualified and already trusting in the quality of your offering and the respectability of your staff.

With a little effort, and the creation of a formalized system – or strategy – you can not only continue to enjoy referral business, but easily double the number of referral customers that walk through your door. All of this is possible for a minimal investment of time and resources.

Is Your Business a Referral Business?

Referral based businesses benefit from a stream of qualified customers who arrive at their doorstep ready to spend. These businesses put less focus on advertising to generate new leads, and more focus on serving and communicating with their existing customers.

Generally speaking, a referral program can generate outstanding results for nearly any business. Since most referrals do not require any effort, the addition of a strategy and a program will often double or triple the number of qualified referrals that come through a business door.

There are, however, a few types of businesses that will not benefit from or do not need a formalized referral strategy. In addition to the big brands, these are more often convenience businesses with low price points – like fast food restaurants and drugstores. Their customer base is broad already, and their efforts would be best spent on increasing the average sale.

A referral program can:

- **Save you time**. Referral strategies – once established – don't require much management or time investment.

- **Deliver more qualified customers**. Your customer arrives with an assumption of trust, and willing to purchase.

- **Improve your reputation.** Your customer's networks likely overlap, and create potential for a single customer to be referred by two people. This encourages the perception that your business is "the place to go."

- **Speed the sales process.** You will have existing common ground and a reputation with the referred customer.

- **Increase your profit.** You will spend less time and money generating leads, and more time serving customers who are ready to buy and want what you have to offer.

The Cost of Your Customers

As we discussed in the "Repeat Business" section, you don't "get" customers, you *buy* them. The money you spend on advertising, direct mail, and other promotions ideally results in potential customers walking through your doors.

For example, if you placed an ad for $200, and 20 people make a purchase in response to that ad, you would have paid $10 for each customer.

Referral customers cost you next to nothing. Your existing customer does the work of selling your business to their friend or associate, and you benefit from the sale. Aside from the cost of any referral incentives or coupon production, there is no cost involved at all.

Referral customers cost less and require less time investment than any other customer. That means you can spend that time making them a loyal customer, or a devoted fan.

Groom Your Customers

Referral strategies can allow you to groom your customer base. As we have previously discussed, 80% of your revenue comes from 20% of your customers (remember the 80/20 rule?) – these are your ideal customers.

These are also the people you have established as your target market, and the people you cater to in your marketing and advertising efforts.

You also have a group of customers who make up 80% of your headaches. These are the people who complain the most and spend the least.

Use your referral strategy to get more of your *ideal* customers. Spend more time servicing your ideal customers – do everything you can to make them happy – and less time on your headache customers. You can even ask your headache customers to shop elsewhere.

Then, focus your referral efforts on your ideal customers. Ask them to refer business to you, and reward them for doing so. Try to avoid referrals from your headache customers – chances are you'll just get another headache. If they're not championing you like a true ambassador, then the quality of the referrals can reflect that. I have had very high-quality clients bringing referrals to me and it was always the most rewarding experience.

Referral Sources

Take some time to brainstorm all the people who could potentially refer business to you. Think beyond your business, to your extracurricular activities and personal life. There are endless sources of people who are ready and willing to send potential customers your way. Always, whenever you are asking for something, be sure to ask what you might do for them. Make sure that they know that they can call on you, too.

Here are some ideas to get you started:

Past Relationships

No, not romantic relationships, unless these have shifted into solid friendships. I'm talking about anyone you have previously had a relationship with, but for one reason or another have fallen out of touch. This includes former colleagues, associates, customers and friends.

Including them in your referral strategy can be as simple as reaching out through the phone or email, and updating them on your latest business initiative or career move. Gently ask at the end of the correspondence to refer anyone who may need your product or service. They will appreciate that you have attempted to re-establish the relationship.

Suppliers and Vendors

Your suppliers and vendors can be a great source for referrals, because they presumably deal daily with businesses that are complementary to your own. The opportunities to connect two of their customers in a mutually beneficial relationship are endless. These businesses should be happy to help out - especially if you have been a regular and loyal customer.

Customers and Clients

Customers and clients are an obvious source of referrals because they are the people who are dealing with you directly on a regular basis. Often, all you have to do is ask and they will happily provide you with contact information of other interested buyers, or contact those buyers themselves.

Your customers also have a high level of product knowledge when it comes to your business, and are in a great position to really sell the strength of your company. Remember that the words of your customers are at least 10 times more powerful than any clever headline or marketing piece you could create.

Employees and Associates

Give your employees and associates a reason to have their friends and families shop at your business with a simple incentive program. These people have the most product knowledge, and are in the best position to sell you to a potential customer.

This is also a way to tap into an endless network of people. Who do your employees and associates know? Who do their friends and friends of friends know? A referral chain that connects to your employees can be a highly powerful one.

Competitors

This doesn't seem so obvious, but it can work. Your direct competitors are clearly not the ideal source for referrals. However, indirect competitors can refer their clients or potential clients to you if they cannot meet those clients' needs themselves.

For example, if you sell high end lighting fixtures, the low-budget lighting store down the street may be able to refer clients to you, and vice versa. You may wish to offer a finder's fee or incentive to establish this arrangement.

Your Network

Don't be shy about asking your friends and family members for referrals. Too many people do not provide enough information to their inner circle about what they do or what their business does. This doesn't make sense, since these are the people who should be the most interested!

Take time to explain clearly what your business is all about, and what your point of difference is. Then just ask them if they know anyone who may benefit from what you are offering. You could even provide your friends and family with an incentive – a gift, a meal, or a portion of the sale.

Associations + Special Interest Groups

This is another place you likely have a network of people who have limited knowledge about what you do or what your business does. The advantage here is that you have a group of people with similar beliefs and values in the same room. Use it!

The Media

Unless a member of the media is a regular customer of yours, or you are in business to serve the media, this may not seem like an obvious choice either.

The opportunity here is to establish a relationship with an editor or journalist, and position yourself as an expert in your field or industry. These people actually need industry experts to quote when putting their content together. My business partner in my market research company was one such go-to expert and was called on from a variety of publications, including the New York Times, the Wall Street Journal and the Los Angeles Times. Once you are recognized as an expert, the next time they are writing a related story, they see you out to quote you. When their audience reads the story, they will perceive your business as the industry leader.

Referral Strategies

A referral strategy is any system you can put in place to generate new leads through existing customers. The ideal way to do this is to create a system that runs itself! Here are some ideas for simple strategies you can begin to implement into your business immediately.

Just Ask

This may seem simple and obvious, but it's true. And, you may be surprised at how few business owners ever ask their own customers for referrals. Be open with your customers and associates, and simply ask them if they can refer any of their friends or associates to you. Make it part of doing business with you, and your customers will grow to expect the question. Or, let them know in advance that you'll be asking at a later date.

Remember that this can include potential customers – even if they don't buy from you. The reason they chose not to purchase may have nothing to do with your business; any person who has begun to or actually done business with you can refer to you another person.

Offer Incentives

When you speak to your customers, when you ask them for something, you typically try to answer the question "what's in it for me?" before they ask it.

The same is true when you ask your customers for a referral. Incentive-based referral strategies work wonders, and can easily be implemented as part of a customer loyalty program, or as part of your existing customer relations systems.

Consider offering customers who successfully refer clients to you discounts on products, free products or services, or gifts. Offer incentives relative to the number of referrals, or the success rate of each referral.

This can have a spin-off effect, as your referral customers may become motivated to continue the referral chain. They too will be interested in the incentives you have provided, and tell their friends about your business.

Be Proactive

The only way your referral program will work is if you put some effort into it, and maintain some level of ongoing effort. Make it a formal program with clarity and structure and it will become easier over time.

Here are some ideas:

- Put a referral card or coupon in every shopping bag that leaves your store
- Promote gift certificates during peak seasons
- Offer free information seminars to existing customers, and ask them to bring a friend
- Host a closed-door sale for your top 20 customers and their friends

Provide Great Customer Service

An easy way to encourage referral business is to treat every potential customer with exemplary customer service. Since the art of customer service is lost in many communities, people are often impressed by simple added touches and conveniences. That alone will encourage them to refer your business to their network.

Stay in Touch

Make sure you are staying in touch with all of your potential and converted customers. Through newsletters, direct mail, or the Internet, keep your business name at the top of the minds of your customers, ahead of the competition.

Even if they have already purchased from you, and may not need to purchase for some time, a newsletter or email can be a simple reminder that your business is out there. If someone in their network is looking for the product or service, it will be more likely that your customer will refer your business over the competition.

I cannot stress enough how lucrative, productive and high value this strategy can be for your business. I have seen it work over and over in my own businesses and in my clients' companies.

6

Profits Are Even More Important than Revenue

As a small business owner, you are in business for one reason: to make money. If it was about service, then it would be much easier to just get a job.

Of course, there are other reasons you started or purchased your company. You may love the product you sell, or service you provide. You may love the challenge of turning a floundering company into an overnight success. You may just love being your own boss.

Naturally, this all means little if you are not generating enough income to support yourself and your family, as well as the people who work for you, and giving those you love the lifestyle that you all desire.

Nearly all businesses make money. Unless not a single product or service is sold, there is always money coming in. But there is also always money going out. Supplies, wages, marketing, acquisitions and operations all contribute to the expense of just staying in business.

Simply put, profit is the difference between money in and money out. This is the dollar value of your sales, minus the cost of those sales.

In business, you will find that everyone wants to make more money. They want to increase their sales, and bring in more money. **What often gets overlooked is that the true secret to making more money is not increasing sales, but increasing profit.**

What is Profit?

Before you can take steps to increase the profitability of your business, you have to have a solid understanding of:

- types of profit
- what factors influence profit
- what your profit is *right now*

Types of Profit

There are two main types of profit:

Gross Profit

Gross profit is the simplest form of calculating profit. It is simply the money that comes through the cash register, minus the cost of acquiring or providing the products or services.
The formula is:

Total revenue (sales) – cost of goods or services sold = Gross Profit

Net Profit

Net profit is a more accurate reflection of your income. It is calculated by taking your gross profit minus expenses over a specific time period (most often on a quarterly basis).

The formula is:

Gross profit – expenses (cost of running a business) = Net Profit

Factors that Influence Profit

Profit is your bottom line. It is the number that falls out the bottom when all other costs and expenses have been taken into consideration. Do you know what contributes to the amount of profit your business ends up with?

There are three main factors that influence profit:

Sales – Your Conversion Rate

The first and most obvious factor is the money that comes in the door through sales. In theory, the more sales you make, the more money you bring in, the greater your profits, depending of course on pricing, discounts offered, and costs associated with bringing in additional revenue, among other factors.

The ratio of potential customers to sales is called your conversion rate. This is the percentage of customers you have converted from leads to sales. So, a high conversion rate means more sales, and more money coming in the door.

In addition to your conversion rate is the lifetime value of your clients. It costs much less to convince a customer to make repeat purchases than it does to acquire new clients.

Costs – Your Product/Service Margins

The second factor is the cost of your offering – what your product or service costs you to acquire or provide. If you sell a product, this is the wholesale price you pay for the product. If you offer a service, it is the cost of your (or your employee's) time plus any materials used.

Your margin is the difference between the price you pay and the price your customers pay. If you buy toothpaste for $1 from the wholesaler, and you sell it for $3, your margin is $2. If a haircut costs $20 in materials and service, and the customer pays $50, your margin is $30.

Expenses – The Cost of Doing Business

The final factor is the cost of running your business – those not directly related to the specific product or service you offer. Expenses include:
- Office or store lease
- Computer equipment lease
- Employee salaries
- Utilities
- Marketing + advertising

Your Profit

It only makes sense that you need to know where you are to determine how to get to where you want to be. This applies to any plan to create or assess a business. And that's why we have this Roadmap!

Before you can increase your profits, you need to have an understanding of where your profits are currently – and if you're making any at all. The next section will take you through a process to review the specific factors that affect your business's profitability, and ultimately determine how much profit you are currently bringing in.

Taking Stock of Your Profits

Before you devise a strategy to increase your profits, you need to take a good long look at the money your business brings in, and the money you spend to run your business. You may need to sit down with your accountant or bookkeeper to analyze the financial information that is available to you, if you are not well and consistently versed on your numbers.

Decide on a specific time period to review – one that makes sense to your business, and one that will give you the most realistic picture of your business performance.

This will depend on whether your operation is cyclical, or remains steady throughout the year. Usually, the previous quarter or the previous four quarters will give you enough of an indication.

Here is a general list of items to review:

- Total revenue
- Total cost of goods or services
- Total cost of operations (overhead), including:
- Employee wages
- Recruitment
- Business development
- Utilities
- Rent or mortgage
- Office supplies
- Computer leases
- Incidentals
- Total cost of marketing campaigns

Total profit after costs and expenses for this time period: $_____.

The Five Factors that Eat Your Profits

It is easy for business owners to compare their organizations to the apparent success of their competitors. Joe's Pizza may always be teeming with customers and appearing to be making money hand over fist, while your pizza shop may have slower, but more steady business.

It is important to remember that a business with extraordinary sales figures is not necessarily a profitable one. Sales are just one element of your profit calculation.

Here are some other elements to think about when reviewing the profitability of your business:

Impulse Spending

How often do you make purchases for your business operations? I'm not talking about acquiring new goods and services, but upgrading computers, taking your team out for lunch, or leasing a new color photocopier.

Do you allow your staff to make purchases on your behalf? Who reviews these decisions? Take a look not only at *what* you buy, but *how* spending is structured in your company.

Small Margins

As we discussed in the previous section, your margins are the difference between your cost and the customer's cost to purchase your goods or services.

Typically, businesses that offer a variety of products will have both products with large margins, and products with small margins. The products with large margins generate the most income, so these are the products that staff should be focused on selling.

What many businesses overlook is that products with small margins will never generate a high level of income, no matter how many you sell. A store stocked with small margin items will never be able to increase their profit because they have so little margin to work with.

In my businesses, I was constantly analyzing gross profit margins to determine what products we should be focusing on to increase margins and profitability. This was particularly important when we needed to make capital investments – if you are reinvesting your profits to grow the business, you will need to come up with additional cash flow at any number of junctures. Where will this come from? Increasing sales of low-margin products and services will not necessarily serve you as well as the high-margin sales in being able to make capital expenditures.

Your Customers

This may seem like a backwards way of thinking. Your customers spend money, so they are a positive factor in your profit calculation, right?

This is true for most of your customers. But remember the 80/20 rule of business – 80% of your revenue comes from 20% of your customers. These are your top 20%, or ideal customers. What about your bottom 20%? The group of clients who ask for the moon and never stop complaining.

These clients can be a huge drain on both your staff resources and your financial resources. Their true value to your business is minimal – they cost more than they bring in. Fire them!

Loan Interest

How many business loans do you currently have? Credit card debit? Overdraft? The interest you pay on these loans can be a substantial monthly cost to your business.

A loan from a bank is just like any other product. You can shop around for the best deal. Consider consolidating or restructuring your debit to minimize interest payments. Plan to search around for the best rate on a regular basis – every few months or quarter.

Vendors

Do you purchase your goods and services from a wholesaler or retailer? How long have you been in business with this company? What do you pay for goods and services relative to your competitors?

Ensure that you are dealing with as direct a vendor as possible to minimize your acquisition costs and increase your margins. If you have been doing business with a particular vendor for an extended period of time, consider renegotiating your business arrangement.

One company that I owned and ran included a retail operation. Because we were small, and offered convenience for a high-value activity, we could afford to pay "Bigbox" retail prices for certain commonly-sold items and resell them at a premium to our customers who didn't mind and actually expected to pay for the convenience. Knowing when this makes sense will help increase profitability.

The Basics of Increasing Profit

Your Profitability Goal

Now that you have an understanding of the current profitability of your company, it is time to look at ways to increase your bottom line.

Like all other aspects of your business development, you need to have a clear idea of your intention or purpose before you begin any activity. Assuming you wish to increase the profitability of your business, you need to determine by how much and within what time frame.

Create a profit-related goal for your business, and write it here:

_____

_____

Three Ways to Increase Profit

There are countless strategies for increasing profit, but ultimately you can only increase profit through sales in one of three ways:

1. Get More Customers

Use marketing outreach strategies to generate more leads, and convert those leads into more customers. Introduce a new offer, expand your target audience, or approach a new target audience.

2. Get Your Customers to Buy More Often

Use customer loyalty and retention strategies to get your existing customers to buy from you more often. Make it easy for them to come back and do business with you.

You can do this by adding value to your product or service with innovation, keeping in touch on a regular basis, and giving your customers incentive to make repeat purchases. Customer service is also an overlooked component of building a repeat client base.

3. Increase How Much Your Customers Buy

You'll naturally increase your sales when you increase the number of customers and how often they purchase. The final way you can impact your profit is by increasing the average dollar value of each sale.

This can be achieved by up-selling every customer, creating package offers, and finding ways to increase the perceived value of your offering to justify increasing the price. Do not be afraid to increase prices. If you can create higher perceived value for your customers, they will be willing to pay the higher price.

Managing Costs

One important way to impact the profitability of your business is through cost or spending management. Controlling how much money goes out will help you ensure that more money stays in your bank account.

Remember, however, that cutting costs can only help increase your profits so much. There is a point where you will no longer be able to reduce expenses, and you will have to focus on increasing sales.

Why Cut Costs?

Cost management may seem like an obvious way of maintaining a healthy business, but it is also one of the primary reasons 80% of small businesses fail. Overspending is a huge problem for most businesses – and they don't even realize it. The key is finding the right balance of saving costs and spending to increase revenue. In one of my rapid-growth businesses, we had a philosophy to not hire new employees during the "highs" in our business. It kept our payroll, the highest expense in our business, to as lean a budget item as possible while continuing to grow our revenues. That strategy had a limit though, in terms of how fast and far the business could grow.

Reducing costs is a great short-term strategy to boost profits. As I mentioned above, there is a limited amount of impact cost management can have on the bottom line, so it is an ineffective long term strategy.

Cost management can also help you to generate more capital. A business that closely monitors and controls its spending is a much more desirable loan candidate than a business that spends freely.

93

Most importantly, this strategy will help keep your business profitable through high and low periods. It's easy to spend money when your company is doing well, but this leaves little in the "just in case" account for downturns in the economy or unexpected expenses. If you manage cash well during the high periods, you will be able to create a contingency budget and be better prepared for the low periods. I have always spun off a fixed percentage of profits to a contingent fund whenever possible, during the high flow periods.

Where Can I Cut Costs?

Financing

As I mentioned, interest rates are a big culprit when it comes to eating profits. Take stock of how much money you are spending on a monthly basis in loan and interest payments. Can this be reduced? Is there another bank that will offer you a lower rate? Is there a way to consolidate these loans into a single, low-interest account?

Alternatively, if your business is doing well and has a large amount of money sitting in the bank; consider investing it or placing it in a high-interest savings account. Let your money make you money instead of spending it on unnecessary business luxuries.

Suppliers or Vendors

Again, as mentioned above, make sure the price you pay for goods and services – for resale or internal use – is the lowest you can find. Try to deal directly with the manufacturer or distributor, and renegotiate discounts and contracts with your vendors every year.

Hours of Operation

Evaluate the hours you are open for business each day, and why you have chosen the specific timeframe. Is it to compete with the competitors? Is it because you can serve the highest number of customers? Each hour you are open for business costs your business money, so make sure you are operating under the most ideal timeframe.

Staffing, Wages, and Compensation

This can be a sensitive subject for any business owner or employee. It is important to look at staffing redundancies and capacity levels – as well as hiring needs – when evaluating cost management strategies.

Do you need to hire new staff, or can you build capacity within your existing employees? Is there another way to compensate staff, or provide performance incentives that are non-monetary, have a high perceived value, and are inexpensive for your business? In the entertainment industry, year-end gift-giving is very customary and expected – it was a significant budget item on our P/L. During lean years, we had to be more selective about which clients would get what gifts and we used charitable donations quite liberally.

Remember to take time and care when implementing any changes in this area of cost management.

Place of Business

If you operate an office in a downtown metropolis, you are going to have substantially higher operating costs than a competitor who runs an office just outside the city limits.

Make sure you can justify your location, and the amount of money you spend to be there. Consider the following questions:

- Are my customers impacted by where I do business?
- Do my customers need to visit my office?
- What impression does my business need to present?
- Do I need parking facilities?
- Do I need to be visible?
- Do I have staff to employ?
- Am I near public transit, lunch outlets, and other amenities?
- Do I need access after business hours?
- Should I lease or buy?
- What other costs are specific to this location?

Eliminate the invisible!

What could you and your staff live without? What wouldn't you notice if it just disappeared one day? Take stock of expenses that are not being properly used or appreciated. Think of amenity-based items, or convenience costs, like:

- Gym Memberships
- Morning refreshments (muffins, donuts, etc.)
- Publication Subscriptions
- Designer coffee and tea
- Fancy collateral packaging

Your Pricing Strategy

The cost of your goods and services have a direct impact on the money you bring in. Your pricing strategy is so important to your business that it can even determine your success.

Deciding how much to charge for your product or service is a challenging task. You need to factor in your own costs, the product or service's perceived value, and the going rate. Ultimately, you want to be able to charge as much as possible for each item, without overpricing yourself out business.

Avoid the Lowest Pricing Strategy

The days of the lowest price guarantee and pricing wars are over – especially for small businesses. The "big players" in the marketplace will quickly put you out of business if you try to compete on price. Their pockets are deeper and they have lower operating costs due to their sheer size. They can afford to have losses – you can't.

Clearly Position Your Company and Your Offering

How do you want your target market to view your business, and your products? Are you trying to create an image of high quality? High value? Reliable service? Make sure your pricing is consistent with the image you are trying to project. If you are operating a high-end spa – you're not competing with the budget nail salon down the street, so your prices should be considerably higher.

Have a Good Working Understanding of Your Margins

Know how much the product or service costs you to offer before you establish a price. Do these costs remain consistent, or do they fluctuate? Restaurants that offer high quality meat and seafood often price their meals at "market rates" as opposed to fixed rates. Calculate the fixed and variable costs associated with your product or service. You will want to work the cost of the product or service, a percentage of your overhead, and your own profit into determining the price of each item.

Pay Attention to Factors Beyond Your Control

Be aware of any government or industry regulations on the price of your product or services. Some laws will actually limit how much you can charge for standard services. For medical and dental services, most insurance companies will put a cap on how much a customer will be compensated for each service. Seek out all external factors that could impact your pricing.

Price with a Purpose

Your pricing strategy should be purpose focused. What exactly are you trying to do by setting your prices at certain levels? Here are some potential reasons for pricing strategies:

- Short-term profit increase
- Long-term profit increase
- Customer generation
- Product positioning
- Revenue maximization
- Increase margins
- Market differentiation
- Survival

Pricing Strategies

Cost Plus Pricing

This is the most basic pricing strategy. Set your price at a number that includes:

- Cost of goods or services, based on a specific sales volume
- Percentage of expenses
- Profit margin (markup)

Target ROI Pricing

Set your price at a rate that will achieve a specific Return on Investment target. If you need to make $20,000 from 1,000 units – or $20 per unit – then set your price at $20 more than cost, plus expenses.

Value Based Pricing

This can be a bit of an arbitrary pricing strategy, but it can also be the most profitable. Set your price based on the value or added benefit it brings to a customer. For example, if your product only costs you $40 to produce, but will save the customer $2,000 per year in energy costs, a price of $150 or $200 would not appear to be unreasonable in the eyes of the customer.

Psychological Pricing

What messages are you trying to send the customer when they're looking at your prices for your products? Do you offer the best deal? The highest value? These are reasons to choose prices that are higher or lower than the competition.

Pricing Guidelines

Price higher than cost. This may seem obvious, but ensure that your pricing not only covers your costs, but potential fluctuations in sales volume and in the marketplace. If you sell half of your order, will you still make a profit?

Include expenses. If you price to cover your costs, will you also be able to cover your expenses and still see a profit? Your margin needs to pay for your expenses, leave you with something to live on, plus some working capital for the company. Consider the seasonality of your products or services and whether there is enough profit from the high season to sustain throughout the low seasons.

Consider the 'fair' price. What do your consumers think is 'fair' for each service or product? This is impacted by your competitor's price, your company's image (high quality or high value, low cost), and the perceived value of your product or service.

Strategies to Increase Profit

Once you have a concrete understanding of where your business stands today in terms of profitability, minimized your operating costs, and restructured your pricing strategy, you can focus on other strategies to increase profit.

There are countless strategies and tactics that will help you to bring in more customers, get those customers to come back, and get those customers to spend more when they do.

Here is a list of ideas, many of which are covered in detail in other sections of this program:

- Advertise
- Establish an online presence
- Sell more high margin items
- Generate more leads
- Focus on referral business
- Increase customer loyalty and repeat business
- Increase conversion rates
- Restructure your team
- Reinvent your product
- Sell your intellectual capital

7

Use Goal Setting Effectively

We've all heard about the power of setting goals. Everyone has surely seen statistics that connect goal setting to success in both your business life, and your personal life. I'm sure if I asked you today what your goals are, you could rattle off a few wants and hopes without thinking too long.

However, what most people do not realize is that the power of goal setting lies in *writing goals down*. Committing goals to paper and reviewing them regularly gives you a 95% higher chance of achieving your desired outcomes. Studies have shown that only three to five percent of people in the world have written goals – the same three to five percent who have achieved success in business and earn considerable wealth.

These studies have also found that by retirement, only four per cent of people in the world will have enough accumulated wealth to maintain their income level, and quality of life. As a business owner, it is essential that you develop a plan for your retirement, but it is equally essential that you develop a plan for your success.

This chapter focuses on the power of goal setting as part of your business success. We'll teach you to set SMART goals that are rooted in your own personal value system, and supporting techniques to achieve your goals faster.

What are Goals?

Goals are clear targets that are attached to a specific time frame and action plan; they focus your efforts, and drive your motivation in a clear direction. Goals are different from dreams in that they outline a plan of action, while dreams are a conceptual vision of your wish or desired outcome.

Goals require work; work on yourself, work for your business, and work for others. You cannot achieve a goal – no matter how badly you want it – without being prepared to make a considerable effort. If you are ready to invest your time and energy, goals will help you to:

- Realize a dream or wish for your personal or business life
- Make a change in your life – add positive, or remove negative
- Improve your skills and performance ability
- Start or change a habit – positive or negative

Why Set Goals?

As we've already reviewed, setting goals and committing them to paper is the most effective way to cultivate success. The most important reason to set a goal is **to attach a clear action plan to a desired outcome.**

Goals help focus our time and energy on one (or several) key outcome(s) at a time. Many business owners have hundreds of ideas whirring around in their heads at any one time, on top of daily responsibilities. By writing down and focusing on a few ideas at a time, you can prioritize and concentrate your efforts, avoid being stretched too thin, and produce greater results.

Since goals attach action to outcomes, goals can help to break down big dreams into manageable (and achievable) sections. Creating a multi-goal strategy will put a road map in place to help you get to your desired outcome. If your goal is to start a pizza business and make six figures a year, there are a number of smaller steps to achieve before you achieve your end result.

Success doesn't happen by itself. It is the result of consistent and committed action by an individual who is driven to achieve something. Success means something different for everyone, so creating goals is a personal endeavor. Goals can be large and small, personal and public, financial and spiritual. It is not the size of the goal that matters; what matters is that you write the goal down, that it is measurable, achievable within a realistic time frame, and that you are committed to making the effort required to achieve it.

What happens when I achieve a goal?

You should congratulate yourself and your team, of course! By rewarding yourself and your team after every achievement, you not only train your mind to associate hard work with reward, but develop loyalty among your employees. At my last business, we made a point of rewarding achievements large and small with gestures, bonuses, and thoughtful gifts to acknowledge the effort expended. In response, we developed a highly-committed, hard-working, reliable team.

You should also ask yourself if your achievement can be taken to the next level, or if your goal can be stretched by building on the effort you have already made. Consistently setting new and higher targets will lay the framework for constant improvement and personal and professional growth.

Power of Positive Thinking

When was the last time you tuned into your internal stream of consciousness? What does the stream of thoughts that run through your mind sound like? Are they positive? Negative? Are they logical? Reasonable?

Positive thinking and healthy self-talk are the most important business tools you can ever cultivate; by programming a positive stream of subconscious thoughts into your mind, you can control your reality, and ultimately your goals. Think about someone you know who is constantly negative; someone who complains and whines and makes excuses for their unhappiness. How successful are they? How do their fears and doubts become reality in their world?

You are what you continuously believe about yourself and your environment. If you focus your mind on something in your mental world, it will nearly always manifest as reality in your physical world.

Positive thinking is a key part of setting goals. You won't achieve your goal until you believe that you can. You will achieve your goals faster when you believe in yourself, and the people around you who are helping to make your goal a reality.

Successful people are rooted in a strong belief system – belief in themselves, belief in the work they are doing, and belief in the people around them. They are motivated to improve and learn, but also confident in their existing skills and knowledge. Their positive attitude and energy is clearly felt in everything they do.

Ever notice how complainers usually surround themselves with other complainers? The same is true of positive thinkers. If you cultivate an upbeat and positive attitude, you will be surrounded by people who share your values and outlook on life.

Too often, people and our society subscribe to a continuous stream of negative chatter. The more you hear it, the more you'll believe it.

How many times have you heard:

- That's impossible.
- Don't even bother.
- It's already been done.
- We tried that, and it didn't work.
- You're too young.
- You're too old.
- You'll never get there.
- You'll never get that done.
- You can't do that.

Who among us hasn't been guilty of thinking or saying these kinds of things out loud?

I remember dreaming of playing the saxophone when I was a young adult. I told myself that it was too late, I was too old. Fortunately, I happened upon a wonderful instrument and a patient teacher and I gave myself the gift of lessons and permission to try. Because of that experience, it was easier later on, when I wanted to learn to play the ukulele. Anything is possible if you can believe in what you desire.

Positive thinking and positive influences will provide the support you need to achieve your goals. Choose your friends and close colleagues wisely, and surround yourself with positive thinkers. Remember, too, that positive thinking starts from within and take responsibility for your own thoughts and outcomes!

Creating SMART Goals

SMART goals are just that: smart. Whether you are setting goals for your personal life, your business, or with your employees, goals that have been developed with the SMART principle have a higher probability of being achieved.

The SMART Principle

1. Specific

Specific goals are clearer and easier to achieve than nonspecific goals. When writing down your goal, ask yourself the five "W" questions to narrow in on what exactly you are aiming for. Who? Where? What? When? Why?

For example, instead of a nonspecific goal like, "get in shape for the summer," a specific goal would be, "go to the gym three times a week and eat twice as many vegetables."

2. Measurable

If you can't measure your goal, how will you know when you've achieved it? Measurable goals help you clearly see where you are, and where you want to be. You can see change happen as it happens.

Measurable goals can also be broken down and managed in smaller pieces. They make it easier to create an action plan or identify the steps required to achieve your goal. You can track your progress, revise your plan, and celebrate each small achievement. For example, instead of aiming to increase revenue in 2017, you can set out to increase revenue by 30% in the next 12 months, and celebrate each 10% along the way.

3. Achievable

Goals that are achievable have a higher chance of being realized. While it is important to think big, and dream big, too often people set goals that are simply beyond their capabilities and wind up disappointed. Goals can stretch you, but they should always be feasible to maintain your motivation and commitment.

For example, if you want to complete your first triathlon but you've never run a mile in your life, you would be setting a goal that was beyond your current capabilities. If you decided instead to train for a five-mile race in six months, you would be setting an achievable goal. You can build towards that triathlon as you expand your goals, while achieving milestones along the way.

4. Relevant

Relevant – or realistic – goals are goals that have a logical place in your life or your overall business strategy. The goal's action plan can be reasonably integrated into your life, with a realistic amount of effort.

For example, if your goal is to train to climb to base camp at Mount Everest within one year and you're about to launch a start-up business, you may need to question the relevance of your goal in the context of your current commitments. And, by the same token, balance in the workplace and in your life can be an important goal, even as you launch a startup. How and what do you need to shift to create something new professionally while also maintaining a balanced life?

5. Timely

It is essential for every goal to be attached to a time-frame – otherwise it is only a dream. Check in to make sure that your time-frame is realistic - not too short, or too long. This will keep you motivated and committed to your action plan, and allow you to track your progress. And know that, if you miss a "deadline" you can always move the timeline out. This has happened to me of course, and in the beginning, I would beat myself up about not meeting the goal, allowing it to become part of my negative self-talk. Once I gave myself permission to hold steady with that "missed" goal, after my timeline for completion had passed, I made that goal achievable, only in a different, much better time-frame, it turned out, in hindsight.

Autosuggestion + Visualization

Autosuggestion and visualization are two techniques that can assist you in achieving your goals. Some of the most well-known and successful people in the world use these techniques, and it is not coincidence that they are masters in their own fields of business and sport. A few of these people include:

- Michael Phelps (Olympic Swimmer)
- Andre Agassi (Tennis)
- Wayne Gretzky (Hockey)
- Bill Gates (Microsoft)

- Walt Disney (Entertainment)

Of course, each of these people have a high degree of talent, ambition, intelligence and drive. However, to reach the top of their respective field, they have each used Autosuggestion and Visualization.

Autosuggestion

Autosuggestion is your internal dialogue; the constant stream of thoughts and comments that flows through your mind, and impacts what you think about yourself and how you perceive situations.

Since you were a small child, this self-talk has been influenced by your experiences and has programmed your mind to think and react in certain ways. The good news is that you can reprogram your mind and customize your self-talk any way you like. That is the power of Autosuggestion.

To begin practicing Autosuggestion, make sure you are relaxed and open to trying the technique; an ideal time is just before bed, or when you have some time to sit quietly. Then, repeat positive affirmations to yourself about the ideal outcome. Top sports and businesspeople will often practice just before a big game or meeting.

Some examples of positive self-talk or autosuggestion include:

- I will lead my team to a victory tonight!
- I will be relaxed and open to meeting new people at the party tonight!
- I will deliver a clear and impacting speech!
- I will stop worrying and tackle this problem tomorrow!

- I will stand up for my own ideas in the meeting!
- I will remember everything I have studied for the test tomorrow!

Visualization

Visualization is a practice complementary to Autosuggestion. While you can repeat affirmations to yourself over and over, combining this practice with visualization is twice as powerful.

Visualization is exactly what it sounds like: repeatedly visualizing how something is going to happen in your mind's eye. Nearly everyone in professional sports practices this technique. It has been proven to enhance performance better than practice alone.

This technique can easily be applied to business. For example, prior to any presentation or meeting where you must speak, present or "perform." I have used this technique when I am about to go on a stage or in front of a group. I have certain practices that I use to create the graceful, fun, impactful experience that I see through visualization.

You can also visualize yourself being incredibly productive and effective in your office. Or, having a discussion with your spouse calmly and rationally.

Elements to think about during visualization:

- What does the room look like?
- What do the people in the room look like?
- What is their mood? How do they receive me?
- What image do I project?
- How do I look?
- How do I behave? What is my attitude?
- What is the outcome?

Give it a try, stay with it and be consistent, and see what results you can create over and over.

8

Effective Systems and Processes Improve Your Bottom Line

One of the biggest mistakes a business owner can make is to create a company that is completely dependent on the owner's involvement for the success of its daily operations. This is called working "in" your business. You're writing basic sales letters, licking stamps, and guiding staff step-by-step through each task. I used to joke that, with my startups, I was the COO, General Counsel and Chief Toilet-Paper-Roll-Changer…except that it wasn't really a joke! That is not a long-term strategy for growth and sustainability. In the beginning, we are willing to do "whatever it takes", and that can work only if it is temporary.

There are a number of problems with this approach for the long-term. One is redundancy. You're paying your staff to carry out tasks that you eventually complete. The second is poor time management. You're spending your day – at your high hourly rate – on tasks as they arise, leaving little room for the tasks you need to be focused on.

However, the biggest issue I have with this approach is that countless intelligent business owners are spending the majority of their time operating their business, instead of *growing* it.

A good test of this is to ask yourself, what would happen if you took off to a hot sunny destination for three weeks and left your cell phone, PDA and laptop at home. Would your business be able to continue operating?

If you said no, then this chapter is for you.

Systemizing your business is about putting policies and procedures in place to make your business operations run smoother – and more importantly – without your constant involvement. With your newfound free time, **you will be able to focus your efforts on the bigger picture: strategically growing your business. You may even get to head to that sunny destination without your cell phone!**

Why Systemize?

For most small business owners, systems simply mean freedom from the day-to-day functioning of their organization. The company runs smoothly, makes a profit, and provides a high level of service – regardless of the owner's involvement.

Systemizing your business is also a healthy way to plan for the future. Hopefully, you will not be working forever – what happens if and when you retire? How will you transition your business to new ownership or management? How will you take that vacation you've been dreaming of?

I've actually had a client tell me that his exit strategy was to work until he died. If that's not how you would like to spend your waning days, then read on.

Businesses that function without their ownership are also highly valuable to investors. Systemizing your business can position it in a favorable light for purchase, and merit a higher price tag.

A system is any process, policy, or procedure that consistently achieves the same result, regardless of who is completing the task.

Any task that is performed in your business more than once can be systemized. Ideally, the tasks that are completed on a cyclical basis – daily, weekly, monthly, and quarterly – should be systemized so much so that anyone can perform them.

Systems can take many forms – from manuals and instruction sheets, to signs, banners, and audio or video recordings. They don't have to be elaborate or extensive, but just provide enough information in step-by-step form to guide the person performing the task.

Benefits of Business Systems

There are unlimited benefits available to you and your business through systemization. The more systems you can successfully implement, the more benefits you'll see.

- Better cost management
- Improved time management
- Clearer expectations of staff
- More effective staff training and orientation
- Increased productivity (and potentially profits)
- Happier customers (consistent service)
- Maximized conversion rates
- Increased staff respect for your time
- Increased level of individual initiative
- Greater focus on long-term business growth

Taking Stock of Your Existing Systems

The first step in systemizing your business is taking a long look at the existing systems (if any) in your business. At this point, you can look for any systems that have simply emerged as "the way we do things here."

How does your staff answer the phone? What is the process customers go through when dealing with your business? How are employees hired? Trained? How is performance reviewed and rewarded?

Some of your systems may be highly effective, and not require any changes. Others may be ineffective and require some reworking. If you have previously established some systems, now is a good time to check-in and evaluate how well they are functioning. Don't be afraid to get input from your team. They are usually full of ideas and their perspective is unique.

Use the following chart to record what systems currently exist in your business.

Existing Systems

	Administration	Financials	Communication	Customer Relations	Employees	Marketing	Data

Seven Areas to Systemize

There is no doubt that system creation – especially when none exist to begin with – is a daunting and time-consuming task. For many businesses, it can be difficult to determine where to start to make the best use of their time from the onset.

Here are seven main areas of your business you can to systemize. Begin with one area, and move to the other areas as you are ready. Alternately, start with one or two systems within each area, and evaluate how those new systems affect your business. Each business will require its own unique set of systems. Choose the system(s) that you believe will most immediately impact your bottom line, or give you the greatest amount of freedom to focus on strategy and growth, whichever you consider the highest priority.

1. Administration

This is an important area of your business to systemize because administrative roles tend to see a high turnover. A series of systems will reduce training time, and keep you from explaining how the phones are to be answered each time a new receptionist joins your team.

Administrative Systems	
Opening and closing procedures	Filing and paper management
Phone greeting	Workflow
Mail processing	Document production
Sending couriers	Inventory management
Office maintenance (watering plants,	Order processing
emptying recycle bins, etc.)	Making orders

One of my pet peeves is to see that there are no papers (or emails) lying around in the "inbox" of the office. You can only imagine the huge efficiencies you implement just by creating a system for filing. In my last office, I ran a multi-million-dollar business with a desk with no drawers. And I made sure that my department never had a large pile-up of filing. If these things aren't handled in a systemic way, it can cause a huge slowdown when you actually need to find that one important piece of paper, living in the middle of a pile of as-yet-unfiled papers.

2. Financials

This is one area of systems that you will need to keep a close eye on – but that doesn't mean you have to do the work yourself. Financial management systems are everything from tracking credit card purchases to invoicing clients and following up on overdue accounts.

These systems will help to prevent employee theft, and allow you to always have a clear picture of your numbers. It will allow you to control purchasing, and ensure that each decision is signed-off on.

120

Financial Systems	
Purchasing	Profit / loss statements
Credit card purchase tracking	Invoicing
Accounts payable	Daily cash out
Accounts receivable	Petty cash
Bank deposits	Employee expenses
Cutting checks	Payroll
Tax payments	Commission payments

In the early stages of a young business, cash flow can be very tight, and juggling growth while revenue/profitability is slim can be overwhelming. It is critical that you have a good handle on your cash flow. Having a good system in place can allow you to take your own eyes of the payables and receivables while also knowing your cash position at all times if you have a well-trained, reliable staff.

3. Communications

Communication is essential and time consuming for any business. Fax cover letters, sales letters, internal memos, reports, and newsletters are among the many items that need to be created regularly by different people in your organization.

Most of the time, these communications aren't much different from one to the next, yet each are often created from scratch by a different person. There is a huge opportunity for systemization in this area of your business. Systemized communication ensures consistency and company differentiation. Taking a "template" approach to creating these ongoing communications can result in huge efficiencies.

Communication Systems	
Internal memo template	Newsletter template
Fax cover template	Sales letter template(s)
Letterhead template	Meeting minutes template
Team meeting agenda	Report template
Sending faxes	Internal meetings
Internal emails	Scheduling

4. Customer Relations

Customer relations is another important area for systemization. This includes everything the customer sees or touches in your company, as well as any interaction they might have with you or your staff members.

Establishing a customer relations system will also ensure that new staff members understand how customers are handled in *your* business. It will allow you to maintain a high level of customer service, without constantly reminding staff of your policies. It will also ensure that the success of your customer relations and retention does not hinge on you or any other individual salesperson.

Create scripts that your staff can practice and adopt and make their own so that there is consistency in the high quality standards that you maintain for your business.

Customer Relations Systems	
Incoming phone call script	Sales process
Outgoing phone call script	Sales script
Customer service standards	Newsletter templates
Customer retention strategy	Ongoing customer communication
Customer communications templates	strategy
	Customer liaison policy

5. Employees

Create systems in your business for hiring, training, and developing your employees. This will establish clear expectations for the employee, and streamline time consuming activities like recruitment.

Employees with clear expectations who work within clear structures are happier and more productive. They are motivated to achieve 'A' when they know they will receive 'B' if they do. Establishing a clear training manual will also save you and your staff the time and hassle of training each new staff member on the fly. In my businesses, we have spent inordinate amounts of time creating training or position manuals for the teams. It may have been painful early on but most certainly paid off over time as new staff came on board.

Employee Systems	
Employee recruitment	Staff uniforms or dress code
Employee retention	Employee training
Incentive and rewards program	Ongoing training and professional
Regular employee reviews	development
Employee feedback structure	Job descriptions and role profiles

6. Marketing

This is likely an area in which you spend a large part of your time. You focus on generating new leads and getting more people to call you or walk through your doors. These efforts can be systemized and delegated to other staff members.

Use the information in this program to create simple systems for your basic promotional efforts. Done well, and any one of your staff should be able to pick up a marketing manual and implement a successful direct mail campaign or place a purposeful advertisement.

Marketing Systems	
Referral program	Regular advertisements
Customer retention program	Advertisement creation system
Regular promotions	Direct mail system
Marketing calendar	Sales procedures
Enquiries management	Lead management

7. Data

While we like to think we operate a paperless office, often the opposite is true. Your business needs to have clear systems for managing paper and electronic information to ensure that information is protected, easily accessed, and only retained when necessary.

Coming from an entertainment market research business where we dealt with highly-confidential intellectual property, we had to have very detailed systems in place for handling the sensitive content that we worked with on a daily basis, both on paper and electronically. We had to undergo an initial audit of systems just to gain the client's trust and business, as well as ongoing audits to maintain these relationships.

In addition to assisting with client procurement and retention data management systems can also help you keep your office organized. Everyone knows where information is to be stored, and how it is to be handled, which prevents big stacks of paper piling up with no place to go.

Ensure that within your data management systems, you include a data backup system. That way, if anything happens to your server or computer software, your data – and potentially your business – is protected.

Data Management Systems	
IT Management	Client file system
Data backup	Project file system
Computer repairs	Point of sale system
Electronic information storage	Financial data management

Implementing New Systems

If you completed the exercise earlier in this chapter, you will have a good idea of the systems that are currently in place in your business. The next step is to determine what systems you need to create in your business.

To do this you will need to get a better understanding of the tasks that you and your employees complete on a daily and weekly basis. If you operate a timesheet program, this can be a good source of information. Alternately, ask staff to keep a daily log for a week of all the tasks they contribute to or complete. Doing so will not only give you valuable insight into how they spend their time on a daily basis, but also involve them in the systemizing process.

Review all task logs or timesheet records at the end of the week, remove duplicates, and group like tasks together. From here you can categorize the tasks into business areas like the seven listed above, or create your own categories.

Then, you will need to prioritize and plan your system creation and implementation efforts. Choose one from each category, or one category to focus on at a time. The amount you can take on will depend on your business needs, and the staff resources you have available to you for this process.

You may find, for example, greater efficiencies in employee positions. In my last business, we employed 150 people. Often, there were redundancies of tasks and responsibilities, sometimes necessary and sometimes not. Knowing how to make the most of your resources is a huge benefit that you can create by doing these exercises.

Remember that system creation is a long-term process – not something that will transform your business overnight. Be patient, and focus on the items that hold the highest priority.

Creating Your Systems

There are a variety of ways you can create systems for your business – depending on the type of system you need and the type of business you operate. Some systems will be short and simple – i.e., a laminated sign in the kitchen that outlines step-by-step how to make the coffee – while others will be more complex – i.e., your sales scripts or letter templates.

One thing all of your systems have in common is steps. There is a linear process involved from start to finish. Begin by writing out each of the steps involved in completing the task, and provide as much detail as you can.

Then, review your step-by-step guide with the employee(s) who regularly complete the task and gather their feedback. Once you have incorporated their input, decide what format the system needs to be in: manual, laminated instruction sheet, sign, office memo, audio/video etc.

Testing Your Systems

Now that you have created a system, you will need to make sure that it works. More specifically, you need to make sure that it works without your involvement.

Implement the new system for an appropriate period of time – a week or month – then ask for input from staff, suppliers and vendors, and customers. Evaluate if it is informative enough for your staff, seamless enough for your suppliers, and whether or not it meets or exceeds your customer's needs.

Take that feedback and revise the system accordingly. For more complex systems, you should not expect to get the system right the first time – so be patient.

Systems will also need to be evaluated and revised on a regular basis to ensure your business processes are kept up to date. Structure an annual or bi-annual review of systems, and stick to it.

Employee Buy-In

It will be nearly impossible for you to develop effective systems without the involvement and input of your employees. These are the people who will be using the systems, and who are completing the tasks on a regular basis without systems. They have a wealth of knowledge to assist you in this process.

Employees can also draft the systems for you to review and finalize. This will make the systemization process a much faster and more efficient one.

It is also important to note that when you introduce new systems into your company, there may be a natural resistance to the change. People – including your employees – are habitual people who can become set in the way they are used to doing things. Involving them in the process of creating your systems will result in greater buy-in and adoption of the new systems. Not to mention, when a new hire comes in, the job of training that new hire is made much easier.

Delegation

The final step to systemizing your business is delegation. What is the point of creating systems unless someone other than you can use them to perform tasks?

This doesn't have to mean completely removing your involvement from the process, but it does mean giving your employees enough freedom to complete the task within the structure of the systems you have spent time and considerable thought creating.

After that, allow yourself the freedom of focusing on the tasks that you most enjoy, and that most deserve your time – like creating big picture strategies to grow your business and increase your profits. And maybe even taking that long-awaited and well-deserved vacation!

9

Time Management Leads to More Profits

Manage Time Like Money

Why did you get into business for yourself? Was it to be your own boss? Choose your own hours? Have more time with the family? Spend more time doing what you love? Create financial freedom that you could control? Chances are, you answered yes to all these questions.

These days, you probably wonder where the time went. Why you spend 12 hours at work and barely make a dent in your to-do list. We already know that time is a key resource for you and your business, but it's also a key resource in your life. Harnessing and leveraging time is the only way to enjoy life, and have a profitable business at the same time.

Most business owners carefully manage their financial and personnel resources, and pay due attention to their performance. Marketing plans and budgets are created, people are hired and fired based on performance. What most business owners don't realize is that time – and the time of all employees – requires the same attention and diligent management.

Time will never manage itself. The decision to make a pro-active effort to manage your time must come from you. To make this commitment, it will be helpful to gain perspective on what your time is actually worth and how you are currently spending it. Once you have committed to taking ownership for your own time management, there are a host of tools available to you.

What is Your Time Worth?

Ever wonder what your time is actually worth? Here's a quick way to figure it out:

Target annual income	A.
Working days in a year	B. 235
Working hours in a day	C. 7
Working hours in a year	D. 1,645
A ÷ D = YOUR HOURLY WORTH (before tax + expenses)	E.

This is a very simple calculation intended to put your time in perspective. In reality, no one is productive for each of the 1,645 hours. Even for professionals who bill at hourly rates for their time, it is unlikely that you will actually accumulate this level of productivity on an hour-by-hour basis. Various studies have put actual productivity at anywhere between 25 minutes and four hours per day. Either way, there's a lot of room for improvement.

Let's look at it another way:

Your age	A.
Days in a year	B.
Days spent on earth to date (A x B)	C.
Average life expectancy	D. 70
Total projected days on earth (D x B)	E.
Estimated days left (E – C)	F.

This exercise isn't intended to scare you, but bring your attention to the importance of choosing how you spend each hour you have available. It is a choice! By developing the skills required to manage your time, you will not only have a profitable business, but a rewarding and balanced life.

The Five Culprits of Time Theft

Chances are – if you're like most people – you have no idea where your time goes. You're likely frustrated by the fact that you can spend 10, 12, even 14 hours a day working, and can't seem to make a dent in your to-do list, or only bill half of those hours.

When we're too busy and overloaded with work, we often switch into reactive mode. We can't make it to the bottom of the pile, and end up handling issues and making decisions at the last minute. One of the great benefits of choosing to become proactive in time management is that you can become proactive in all other areas of your business. When in proactive mode, you can take steps to grow your business through networking, building programs, and establishing systems.

Before you investigate where your time goes, let's take a look at the top five culprits of modern-day time theft:

1. Your Email

How many times a day do you check your email? Is Outlook or Mail constantly running on your desktop? Email – internal, external, personal and business – clogs up your day like no other communication channel. For many of us, it is possible to spend the entire day writing and responding to emails without even glancing at our inbox. The number of emails sent and received each day by the average person in 2007 was 147. Multiply that by an average of two minutes per message, and you have spent almost five hours on email in a single day. I know I've been guilty of spending a half a day not taking my eyes of my email account, getting up hours later and realizing that all I had accomplished to that point was dealing with emails. Can you relate?

2. Your Cell Phone

Cell phones and tablets have created convenience, security, and the luxury of telecommuting – but they don't call it a Smartphone for no reason. Smartphones and tablets have also created a society that expects to be able to reach you at any moment, or at least receive instant responses to their calls. Your smartphone and other personal digital devices not only rob you of your time during the day, but also during the evenings and on weekends when you are not at work, as well as on vacation where you are not supposed to be at work. I've had businesses that, to my clients at least, required that I be available 24/7, especially in the early years. I never went on a vacation or to a funeral, or anything in between where I wasn't accessible and responsive.

3. Your Open Door Policy

If you make it easy for your staff and associates to interrupt you, they will. Too often, open-door policies are set up by human resource departments to create clear communication channels. Instead, they create a clog of employees lined up at your door seeking immediate answers to non-emergent issues.

4. Meetings

How many times have you been to a meeting that was scheduled to be an hour, and ended up lasting three? How often do you attend unnecessary meetings? Or meetings that run off-topic? Meetings can be a huge source of wasted time – your valuable time. In a senior management or ownership position, your day may consist of back-to-back meetings, leaving only your evening hours to complete the tasks that should have been done during the day. As a business leader, you have the power to evaluate each meeting that you schedule or are invited to, to decide whether it is an essential use of your time. You can give yourself permission to consider other ways to accomplish the goal of the proposed meeting.

5. YOU!

Every person has daily habits that sabotage their ability to work productively and efficiently. Many entrepreneurs and business owners can't separate business hours from leisure hours. Some get caught in a time warp while surfing the internet. Others - mainly overachievers – can become paralyzed by perfectionism or procrastination. Mainly we just don't have the tools to schedule and structure our time in a way that fits with our working style, and also creates balance in the life.

Where Does Your Time Go?

So far we've seen that time is a resource that should be as carefully managed as cash. We've figured out what your time is worth, and looked at the top five culprits of time theft. You've committed to taking steps to become a better time manager. What now?

Personal Time Management Research Exercise

The next step is to take a good, (and honest!) look at how you spend your time. Once you understand your patterns and habits, you can begin to implement the strategies in this chapter that will make you a better time manager.

Step One: Time Audit

Use the Time Log Worksheet at the back of this chapter to record how you spend your time for three working days in a row. Be honest, and be specific. Include time spent in transit, surfing the web, interacting with clients and colleagues, as well as how your time is spent at home in the evenings. The more information you can record, the easier it will be to analyze your time management skills in step two.

Step Two: Time Categorization

Once you have recorded your time for three days, sit down with all three sheets in front of you and identify the following using different colored markers or highlighters:

- Driving, public transportation or other travel
- Eating, including food preparation
- Personal Errands
- Exercise
- Watching TV
- Sleeping, including naps
- Using the computer, personal use only
- Being with family / friends
- Emailing, including checking, reading, and returning messages
- Talking on the phone, including checking and returning messages
- Internal meetings
- External meetings
- Administrative work
- Client work
- Non-client, non-administrative work

Step Three: Time Analysis

Now that you have identified how you have spent your time, go through the worksheets one more time and identify if you have spent enough, too much, or too little time on each main task.

Then, based on your observations, answer the following questions:

1. What patterns do you notice about how you spend your time during the day? (i.e., When are you most productive? Least productive? Most or least interrupted?)

_____

_____

_____

_____

_____

_____

_____

_____

_____

2. Write down the four highest priorities in your life right now. Does your timesheet reflect these priorities?

_____

_____

_____

_____

_____

3. If you have more time, what would you do?

_____

_____

_____

_____

_____

4. If you had less time, what wouldn't you do?

_____

_____

_____

_____

5. Could you remove the items in question four and add the items in question three? Why or why not?

_____

_____

_____

_____

_____

6. Is procrastination a problem for you? How much?

_____

_____

_____

_____

_____

Strategies for Profitable Time Management

There are many ways to curb time theft and refine your time management ability. Through a solid understanding of how you currently spend – and waste – time, you can determine which strategies you need to implement to correct unproductive behavior.

Here are 17 ways you can turn **less** of your time into **more** money:

1. Set Clear Priorities

The foundation of time management is a clear understanding of what your time is best spent on. Once you accept that you can't do everything, you need to decide what needs to be completed now, what can be completed later, and what someone else can complete. Each to-do list you create should be put through this filter, and reorganized so the highest priority items are on top, and the lowest priority items are less visible, or on the bottom.

Once you have established your priorities – which will also naturally reflect the priorities and goals of your business – stick to them. Just because someone else feels something is of a high priority doesn't mean it holds the same status next to your other tasks.

Prioritization is also helpful in your personal life and leisure time. Your spare time is precious – so make sure you are clear on how you would like to spend it. Remember, too, that time with family and on activities that uplift and energize you, or keep you healthy, should not be dispensable just because they may not be income-producing.

2. Use Your Skills – Delegate Your Weaknesses

As a business owner, your day naturally consists of tasks you dislike doing. Some are essential – signing checks, reviewing financial statements, and other business maintenance – while others are simply not within your skill set.

If you are a strong public speaker, but struggle with report writing – delegate to a copywriter or editor. If you own a retail store and have no experience in design – outsource your signage. These freelance professionals often cost half as much as you, and take half as long to complete the task. Your time is saved for tasks that use and strengthen your skills effectively, your stress is managed, and ultimately a better product is produced.

3. Delegate, Delegate, Delegate

As a small business owner, the only way you will ever get everything done is by delegating. Delegation is a vital skill that needs to be refined and practiced, and once mastered is the key to profitable time management.

Too often, owners and managers believe that it will be "faster" or "more efficient" to complete the task themselves rather than to train and monitor someone else. Other times, there are no internal resources to download assignments to.

As a result, the following trends can be seen in many small companies:

- Owners and senior staff are stressed and overworked, while junior staff are underutilized and under capacity.

- Staff members are not given an opportunity to grow and develop in their roles, and may perceive a lack of trust or confidence in their ability. The company loses good people.

- Owners and senior staff are always in a reactive state, instead of a visionary or proactive state.

- Delegation happens at the very last minute, and junior staff has little understanding of either the overall project or expectations for the task.

The easiest way to fix this problem is before it starts. Create a solid team of staff members around you who are well-trained and prepared to support the business. Attract and retain qualified and quality people who can be cross-trained and promoted within the company. Let them know how much confidence you have in them by involving them in project creation and scope outline. Ensure that communication flows throughout the business, so everyone has the product and service knowledge to step in and assist when necessary.

4. Learn to Say "No"

It's easy to fall into the habit of saying yes to everything. You are, after all the business owner, right? No one can complete these tasks as well as you, right? You'll lose that customer if you don't help them with their garage sale, right?

Wrong. The most successful business owners have a keen understanding of how their time is best spent, and *delegate* the remaining responsibilities to trusted others. It's too easy to say yes to every request in the moment, and later feel overwhelmed when it's added to your to-do list. You may not ruffle any feathers, but what toll does it take on your stress level? Your workload? Your family or free time? Your time is valuable – so protect it!

Remember that if it is too challenging to say no immediately, you can always request some time to think about it. This way, you can evaluate your workload and realistically decide whether or not you can take on a new project. Then, stand by your decision, or assist in bringing in the necessary resources to get it done.

5. Create (and keep!) a Strict Schedule

While multi-tasking is a desirable skill, it is also often a time thief. Attempting to do too many things at one time ensures that nothing gets done. As a business owner, you need to be able to focus and concentrate on essential projects without interruptions.

The only way to do this is to commit to a strict schedule. Once you understand your work style and concentration patterns, you can allocate periods of the day to specific tasks. This includes personal and leisure time – schedule it, and stick to it. This takes discipline and commitment to adhere to. So often we get distracted by the myriad "little things" that we know we can handle and get rid of, but that will divert us from our schedule of other priorities. Pay attention to these distractions and hold yourself accountable. Practice, practice, practice.

Schedule time for: list-creation + prioritization, email messages, telephone messages, internal meetings, client meetings, meeting preparation, "me-time", family time, recreation + fitness, daily business tasks, and blocks for focused work.

Remember that there is a training period involved in beginning a new routine – for yourself and those around you. Use your voicemail, out-of-office email message, and a closed door to begin to let people know when you will not be disturbed.

6. Make Decisions

The choice to not make a decision is a decision in itself. The most successful business owners have the ability to make good decisions quickly and efficiently, and do not waste time deliberating over simple choices.

In leadership positions, often people are afraid of making the wrong decision or looking foolish if they make a mistake in front of junior staff. What they don't realize, is that hesitating or avoiding decision-making impacts their leadership just as much or more than making the wrong decision. Not only can being indecisive be personally stressful, but it is also stressful for those around you whose tasks are waiting on your choices.

Remember, you must make the best decision with the information you have, in the time frame you have to make the decision. No one expects you to be a fortune teller – be decisive, make some mistakes, and learn from them.

7. Manage Telephone/Text/Email Interruptions

This is a huge source of time theft that can easily be managed and avoided. If you are available to take phone calls or respond to text and email messages at any time of day, you are setting yourself up to take work home in the evenings. The phone will always ring and these messages will always come in when you are focused on an important task, and this is something that can easily be avoided.

Figure out when you are most productive. Is it in the morning or the afternoon? Before, during, or after lunch? Once you have identified this time period, set your phone on "do not disturb" or have your calls directed to voicemail. If you do not have a receptionist, a variety of automatic answering systems are available for a nominal fee. To structure your phone time further, let callers know on your voicemail what specific time of day is best to reach you via phone. Then, set that time aside to receive and return phone calls. You can do the same with emails with an outgoing auto-response. And you can simply train and condition people not to expect immediate electronic replies, just because they have reached out.

8. Keep Your Work Environment Organized

Have you ever tried to make dinner in a messy kitchen? More of your time is spent looking for (and cleaning) dishes and tools than actually spent cooking the meal.

The same goes for your work environment. If your desk and office is in a constant state of chaos, then you mind will be too. In fact, some studies have revealed that the average senior business leader spends nearly four weeks each year navigating through messy or cluttered desks, looking for lost information. Does that sound like productive time to you?

Once you make the initial clean sweep, it's easy to maintain order in the chaos:

- Tidy your desk at the beginning and end of each day. Attach pertinent documents to your to do list, or have clear and organized folders for loose papers.
- Organize your supplies drawer so you have easy access to stationery like pens, post-it notes, staplers and highlighters. Every minute counts!

- Only have the documents and files you are working on, on your desk. The rest should be neatly filed on a side table for later retrieval.

- Keep personal items (like photos or memorabilia) out of your primary line of vision. These can be distracting and encourage daydreaming.

As for your office or store, there are many ways to make its layout more conducive to effective time management. Try:

- Minimizing the distance between the reception desk and electronics like photocopies and fax machines.

- Keep a clear line of sight between your office and the most productive area of your business, so you are aware of what is happening amongst your staff.

- Organize shelves and filling cabinets so files are not only easily accessed, but out of sight when not being used. Consider putting sliding doors or cabinets in storage areas, and remember that the floor is not a storage cabinet.

9. Keep Your Filing System Organized

If your data isn't organized properly, you will waste hundreds of hours searching for documents you need on a regular basis. This includes both electronic and hard copy files; they need to be organized and up to date. Remember that just because something has landed in in your inbox, it doesn't mean that you have filed that data away!

Customer databases and inquiry records are worth their weight in gold. You can't afford to get behind when updating this information, or poorly store it for later retrieval. There are many easy to use software programs that will manage and organize customer databases for you; it doesn't need to be a time consuming or tedious exercise.

A simple way to manage information is to keep it in short, medium, and long term files for both hard and electronic copies. Create shortcuts on your desktop for folders or files you constantly access. Have short-term files available on your desk, medium-term files available within an arm's reach, and long-term files stored in cabinets.

10. Clearly Communicate – Never Assume

One of the biggest issues for time management in business – and likely the world – is miscommunication. This is a dangerous issue that can cripple any business, including yours. Establishing and enforcing clear policies on things like accurate note taking, task assignments, and phone messages will ensure your staff understands the importance of clear and accurate communication.

The easiest habit to start to curb miscommunication is simple: write everything down. Carry a notepad or electronic tablet, and jot down key points, figures, agreements and deadlines. Don't assume you'll remember later – you have at least a hundred other things to remember.

Some other simple strategies are:

- Return all communication promptly, including email, letters, faxes and phone calls to the extent these are priorities you've previously established.

148

- Repeat back phone messages, phone numbers and other figures to confirm you recorded the information correctly.

- Record appointments in your PDA or agenda the moment you make them. Otherwise, you will forget.

- Double check and confirm everything – addresses, phone numbers, meeting locations and times.

- Maintain accurate customer contact logs with dates, times, and phone numbers.

- Post checklists in your store or office for routine operations procedures.

- Announce any changes to the policies and procedures manual immediately.

11. Stop Duplicating Efforts

This is a key element of time management that is closely related to effective communication. Studies have continually shown that many businesses often duplicate and triplicate efforts that need only be completed once.

When you have clear systems and procedures in place, your staff will not need to "reinvent the wheel" each time the task needs to be completed. Meeting minutes and individual task assignments will ensure everyone is on the same page and understands their personal responsibilities.

Simple examples of this include re-reading your to-do list each hour to determine what the next important item is. If your list is already structured by priority, this is a needless task. If two staff members are working on similar projects, but unaware of the other, the work will not only be inconsistent, but the efforts will be duplicated. These are easy problems to fix, once they have been identified and communicated.

12. Say Goodbye to Procrastination + Perfectionism

Procrastination is something we all face at one time or another – and likely have since our school days. However, given the pace that the world operates at today, you will only fall behind your competitor if you allow procrastination to rule your day. So how you do avoid it? It's simple. Stop, and just get started, no matter how boring, tedious, or painful the project may be. Reward yourself by crossing each step off your to-do list. Be aware of when procrastination comes from overwhelm of having too much to do. Find a starting point and just dive in, tackling only as much as you can handle in the moment.

Many small business owners also fall victim to perfectionism, which can be paralyzing. The fear that there isn't enough time or resources to "get it perfect" will sometimes stop you dead in your tracks. Perfectionism can also hinder your ability to delegate and say no to tasks you believe no one else can complete "better". Don't let "perfect get in the way of good". Do the best you can with the time and resources you have – and just get started.

13. Plan Your Work, Work Your Plan

Have you ever placed an advertisement on the fly because it was "cheaper", "faster", or "more urgent" than creating a marketing plan? Do you and your staff have a clear idea of where your business is headed over the next six to 12 months, or five years?

Many studies show that less than 10% of small businesses have up to date marketing and business plans, as compared to the majority of large corporations and public companies, which have both.

Marketing and business plans take time and effort to create – but they work, and pay off in spades. They also save you time and money as compared to a haphazard or fly-by-the-seat-of-your-pants strategy. With a marketing plan in place, you will have an idea of how many ads you will be placing in a year, which will earn you a volume discount. Your marketing materials will complement each other, and deliver the same message to the same target audience. Designers will charge less for a package of collateral than for individual collateral items.

A business plan will provide you with a guide to reference when making decisions. You can repeatedly ask if the endeavor at hand will contribute to your overall vision, or just seems like a good idea or price. Each strategy can be measured against the business plan and evaluated as to whether and what impact it will have on the business goals.

Remember that planning includes both short and long-term time frames, and applies to both your daily to-do list, and your marketing budget. It provides you with a means to measure your progress, assists in identifying priorities, and helps to manage your time.

14. Avoid Needless, Impromptu + Unstructured Meetings

This may seem like a time theft issue that is out of your control, but it's not. You are in control of your own time, and through strict scheduling can establish a structure for internal and external meetings that everyone around you can work within. Your hardworking team will also appreciate not being summoned to less-than essential meetings.

Minimize impromptu internal meetings by letting your staff know when you're available for a "quick chat" and when you are not. If it is important, ask them to schedule a time to meet with you that works with both of your schedules. This not only saves you time, but encourages staff to find solutions to their own issues, and only approach you with more urgent or challenging matters.

You can't avoid having meetings, but you can avoid having unstructured meetings. Ask for or create an agenda for each meeting you attend, with a clear objective and an amount of time allocated to each item. This will keep your meetings focused and on task. If a meeting does run late, give yourself a reasonable buffer, and politely leave for your next appointment. You can always follow up with a colleague to catch-up on the pertinent items you may have missed.

15. Establish Clear Policies + Procedures

A clear policy and procedures manual is like a marketing or business plan – it takes time to create, but ultimately saves everyone in your company time, money and effort. A step-by-step guide to "the way we do things here" is an invaluable resource for your existing and new staff, and provides clear expectations for how you like things done.

Too many businesses make up policies and procedures on the fly – creating dangerous scenarios where mistakes are made and expectations are not clear. Some items that should be included in a comprehensive policy and procedures manual include:

- Recruitment
- Customer relations
- Customer inquiries
- Customer complaints
- Returns
- Exchanges
- Late Payments
- Salary structure
- Bonus structure
- Employee review
- Theft
- Harassment

16. Keep the Right Set of Tools

The equipment your business needs to operate (and grow!) effectively should always be on hand, or easily contracted out. This is specific to each company, and closely related to costs – including the cost of your time.

Whether you are a high-tech business or local retailer, knowledge of the latest advancements in technology will increase your efficiency. It will help you stay on top of your competitors, maintain your position as an expert, and perhaps provide an easier way of getting things done.

Always ask yourself if these purchases are essential to your business –could we perhaps make these purchases from a secondhand dealer to minimize cost? Is it more cost effective to outsource or sub-contract the tasks to someone with access to this equipment, or to buy the equipment yourself?

If your business relies on tools and technology for daily tasks (such as various trades professions) then obtaining the best quality tools that you can afford is crucial.

17. Maintain Your Equipment

This may seem obvious, but you'll understand the importance if your network server has ever crashed, or point of sale system has malfunctioned. Your business can be slowed to a stand-still if your equipment is not in good working order. Of course there are instances that can't be predicted, but regular maintenance of your essential equipment will reduce these occurrences and help to anticipate when old equipment needs to be repaired or replaced. One of our businesses was completely dependent on working photocopiers. These machines quite often needed to run 24/7. Because of the nature of the business, we were essentially functioning as a photocopy service to deliver our products to our clients and the time deadlines were critical to the clients. Any malfunction or stoppage of the machines would cause a work stoppage and/or huge premium costs for alternative services. Many businesses have certain essential equipment without which their clients cannot be serviced. Make sure you have implemented all steps necessary to ensure good maintenance strategies and purchasing decisions.

Personal Time Management Strategy

To complete these sections and create a personal time management strategy, make use of the forms provided and do the exercises outlined here. Then, choose the top five tips from this chapter that you think will help you the most, given your personal time management research conducted here. Write them below, with three corresponding actions that you will start tomorrow. For example, if you are going to set a strict schedule, three actions might be to establish the schedule, communicate it to your staff, and re-record your voicemail message.

1. _____

    a._____

    b. _____

    c. _____

2. _____

    a. _____

    b. _____

    c. _____

3. _____

    a. _____

    b. _____

    c. _____

4. _____

    a. _____

    b. _____

    c. _____

5. _____

    a. _____

    b. _____

    c. _____

Timesheet | Day One

Timeslot	Activities	More/Less/ Enough time?
7:00 – 7:30		
7:30 – 8:00		
8:00 – 8:30		
8:30 – 9:00		
9:00 – 9:30		
10:00 – 10:30		
10:30 – 11:00		
11:00 – 11:30		
11:30 – 12:00		
12:00 – 12:30		
12:30 – 1:00		
1:00 – 1:30		
1:30 – 2:00		
2:00 – 2:30		
2:30 – 3:00		
3:00 – 3:30		
3:30 – 4:00		
4:00 – 4:30		
4:30 – 5:00		
5:00 – 5:30		
5:30 – 6:00		
6:00 – 10:00 (Evening)		

Timesheet | Day Two

Timeslot	Activities	More/Less/ Enough time?
7:00 – 7:30		
7:30 – 8:00		
8:00 – 8:30		
8:30 – 9:00		
9:00 – 9:30		
10:00 – 10:30		
10:30 – 11:00		
11:00 – 11:30		
11:30 – 12:00		
12:00 – 12:30		
12:30 – 1:00		
1:00 – 1:30		
1:30 – 2:00		
2:00 – 2:30		
2:30 – 3:00		
3:00 – 3:30		
3:30 – 4:00		
4:00 – 4:30		
4:30 – 5:00		
5:00 – 5:30		
5:30 – 6:00		
6:00 – 10:00 (Evening)		

Timesheet | Day Three

Timeslot	Activities	More/Less/ Enough time?
7:00 – 7:30		
7:30 – 8:00		
8:00 – 8:30		
8:30 – 9:00		
9:00 – 9:30		
10:00 – 10:30		
10:30 – 11:00		
11:00 – 11:30		
11:30 – 12:00		
12:00 – 12:30		
12:30 – 1:00		
1:00 – 1:30		
1:30 – 2:00		
2:00 – 2:30		
2:30 – 3:00		
3:00 – 3:30		
3:30 – 4:00		
4:00 – 4:30		
4:30 – 5:00		
5:00 – 5:30		
5:30 – 6:00		
6:00 – 10:00 (Evening)		

Daily To-Do List | Business

Task	Priority (1-10)	Deadline?	Delegation?

Weekly To-Do List | Personal (Family, Leisure, etc.)

Task	Priority (1-10)	Deadline?	Delegation?

10

Case Studies of Successful Marketing Strategies

The strategies in this program mean absolutely nothing unless you choose to implement them.

The beauty of each of these time-tested strategies is that you can begin implementing them at any time – and start virtually anywhere in the program. There is no need to completely rework your entire marketing campaign or put off making changes until you can make all the changes at once.

This section profiles other business owners who have successfully used the information in this program to grow their businesses.

In each case, it took only a handful of changes to dramatically increase sales, generate higher revenues and increase profitability.

Let their stories motivate you to start working today to improve your own business.

Case Study One

Think Coffee News

Business Type: Small Magazine Publisher

Objective: Increase profits with cross-selling opportunities, without any time expense.

Strategy: Education

Solution(s): A prominent marketing personality was asked to write a regular column and create a series of workshops. The column and workshops were designed to educate clients on easy-to-implement and cutting-edge marketing initiatives, as well as sell clients a twelve-month program (Starter Program).

Value Add Proposition: The twelve-month program would assist advertising clients on marketing their own business, creating better offers, back end sales, as well as profitable joint-venture opportunities.

Method: Free Series of Marketing Workshops + Newsletter Column

Marketing Materials:
- Sales Script to promote Starter Program
- Email template
- Workshop invitation

Result: A sustainable joint venture and cross-selling opportunity was established, and is now worth thousands of dollars in additional revenue per year.

Case Study Two

Young Realtor of the Year

Business Type: Independent Contractor

Issue: Need to increase revenues, but has no extra time available after a successful marketing campaign.

Strategy: Intellectual Capital

Solution(s): When other local realtors phone for free advice, he sells them on shadowing him in action for a day. Less successful realtors ride his coattails for a day and are free to take as many notes as they like. Must guarantee they will not impede his ability to work nor talk to his clients at any stage.

Value Added Proposition: A one-hour debrief is included in the session, plus a hand out to ensure the client experienced/noticed most important parts of day. A less successful realtor is educated, and the young realtor is positioned as an expert through this mentorship program.

Method: Regular, time-consuming phone calls were turned into a source of revenue.

Marketing Materials:
- Sales Script
- Referral Program

Result: Realtor now makes $1,000 per day in addition to successful sales revenues with limited time investment.

Case Study Three

Personal Trainer

Business Type: Independent Contractor

Objective: Need to generate more new leads and create a loyal (more valuable) client base.

Strategy: Risk Reversal and Service Packaging

Solution(s): The personal trainer needed to understand why first-time buyers are reluctant to purchase training services. In response, the first session was offered for free to clients who were qualified through a series of questions. This demonstrated credibility, empathy, insight, and most importantly the ability to provide a benefit to the person. Potential clients had the opportunity to evaluate the service before they opened their wallets.

Value Added Proposition: First session free, with package program of services available for $3,000 for Platinum clients.

Method: Advertise and promote free session

Marketing Materials:
- Training Program
- Sales Scripts
- Referral Program

Result: Personal Trainer tripled industry average revenues with this service package that sold for 10 times the industry average.

Case Study Four

Oil and Gas Company

Business Type: Large-format company

Objective: Need to find a way to keep customers coming back; most customers make 'one-time' purchases of large products that sell for approximately $70,000.

Strategy: Maintenance Program (Service Plan)

Solution(s): Machines sold for $70K and seldom had any issues inside five years. A warranty and Maintenance Program was developed to upsell each client, and provide an opportunity to 'get in the door' of the customer. A condition of the warranty is that the service provider must come in quarterly to service the machine and ensure it was in good health.

Value Added Proposition: The $2,500 maintenance program was up-sold to each customer, providing an (almost) unconditional warranty and ease of mind.

Method: The serviceperson who made quarterly visits to each client also served as a salesperson that would look for other opportunities to provide the client with products or services.

Marketing Materials:

- Collateral for other products
- Sales Script
- Questionnaire

Result: The 'lifetime value' of each client went up dramatically, and most per client sales were increased by $2,500 for the Maintenance Program.

Case Study Five

Accounting Company

Business Type: Service-based Company

Objective: Need to grow business and increase revenues.

Strategy: Education and Expertise Positioning

Solution(s): Educate the market regarding tax strategies 'The Government Doesn't Want You to Know'. Position the business as the experts with cutting edge advice and innovative money saving solutions for clients.

Value Added Proposition: Potential clients were able to gain 'free' information from the business, without making a purchase, which eliminates the risk involved in finding an accountant.

Method: Accountant wrote educational and informative tax columns as well as developed a regular string of seminars.

Marketing Materials:
- Newspaper + Newsletter Columns
- Free Seminars
- Referral Program.

Result: Firmly established themselves as the 'go to' company for businesses looking to pay less tax.

Case Study Six

Music Teacher

Business Type: Independent Contractor

Objective: Need to generate more income to support ambitious business owner.

Strategy: Risk Reversal + Education

Solution(s): Developed a free Loss Leader two-hour group lesson for adults. The most popular song requested was taught, and all participants were guaranteed to be able to play it after the two hours. His clients (adults) were not interested in playing technically well, just in knowing a few songs to play at Christmas, etc.

Value Added Proposition: Clients were not required to put down any money up front, and would have the opportunity to purchase a 12-month training course to continue to develop their skills.

Method: Loss Leader was heavily promoted, and at the end of the session the students were sold a 12-month training course (highly systemized and very little 'time' attached).

Marketing Materials:
- SWOT Analysis
- Advertisements
- Newsletter
- Joint Ventures
- Loss Leader

Result: Licensed his program. He reckons he will have made more money off 'Unchained Melody' than the Righteous Brothers!

Note: This music teacher had a solid back-end 12-month program to sell (very few piano teachers have anything that looks like this). Other teachers will/do have this available to them but will not be savvy enough to capitalize on an opportunity to leverage someone else's program.

Case Study Seven

Lawn Mowing Business

Business Type: Service-based Business

Objective: Find a way to increase revenues and reduce overhead.

Strategy: Competitor Research

Solution(s): Researched the five most successful businesses in their industry. Found the major competitors were companies selling 'licenses' rather than other lawn mowing companies. Created framework of everything needed to 'license'.

Value Added Proposition: Offer $30,000.00 licenses, rather than $50 lawn mowing jobs.

Method: Took everything the company was doing successfully to operate a 'lawn mowing business', and completed manuals for operations and marketing based on existing systems.

Marketing Materials:
- Operations Manual
- Marketing Manuals

Result: Licensed company and tripled previous year's sales with equal or reduced overhead. PLUS: Realized everything that worked for the lawn mowing business could also work, with minor changes, for dog groomers and carpet cleaners. Also licensed these businesses.

Case Study Eight

Community Supermarket

Business Type: Product-based Business

Issue: Needs to find a way to compete with other, larger, grocery stores and stop losing money.

Strategy: Joint Venture Marketing

Solution(s): Create a private label alternative with excellent branding and POS (point of sale) material. Joint venture with other small town supermarkets and ensured long term strategy to 'compete with big boys'.

Value Added Proposition: Huge increases in profit margin for an excellent product

Method: Full blown brand strategy.

Marketing Materials:

- Direct Mail
- Newspaper Ads
- Joint Ventures

Result: 22% increase in profitability.

Case Study Nine

Local Restaurant

Business Type: Service-based Business

Issue: Revenues in a downward spiral.

Strategy: Target Market Research

Solution(s): Restaurant found that their clientele had changed, but they were still modeling their business on what had worked in the past. The name was changed from 'Family Restaurant' to 'Pastaria'; younger staff were recruited; a calendar of events was created to draw crowds; and the brand identity was updated. The new image was one that their desired clientele would resonate with.

Value Added Proposition: Past influential customers were invited to try the revamped restaurant for free (through gift certificates).

Method: Personal letters were mailed to all popular and influential people in the local area (athletes, successful business people, Mayor, Council Representatives, Newspaper publisher, etc.).

Marketing Materials:
- Personal Letters including Gift Certificates
- Calendar of Events
- New brand identity

Result: Revenues tripled over twelve months.

Case Study Ten

Business Incubator

Business Type: Service-based Business

Objective: Increase occupancy in short-term offices and increase profit.

Strategy: Risk Reversal; Powerful Offer

Solution(s): A powerful offer was created and targeted at small to medium sized business owners currently operating from home. The offer included minimal financial investment, ease of transition, and no commitment.

Value Added Proposition: New clients were offered their first month free, no deposit, no contract, and a free moving service. There was no risk involved for the client, and a powerful business operation environment was provided.

Method: Direct mail sales letter to potential business clients who currently operate at home, with follow up calls made by contract salespeople to close the sales.

Marketing Materials:
- Sales Letter
- Sale Script
- Referral Program.

Result; Doubled profits in first year and sustained growth.

Case Study Eleven

Business Incubator

Business Type: Service-based Business

Objective: Business Incubator had developed a system that increased occupancy 22% above industry average (this basically doubled 'profits') and needed to find new ways to grow the business.

Strategy: Purchase Competitors

Solution(s): Developed a list of competitors, and created a financial strategy to acquire them. Most of the business centers jumped at the chance to exit the business as they were operating at industry average. Grew business and market share immediately and also created a viable option for someone looking to sell.

Value Added Proposition: The clients received superior service and were provided with greater leverage through the expanded service centers.

Method: Direct mail piece to all business centers offering to purchase.

Marketing Materials:
- Sales Letter
- Sales Script
- Sales Presentation

Result: Bought several of their competitors, increased market share and brand awareness substantially, profits grew by 75%.

Case Study Twelve

Mortgage Broker

Business Type: Independent Contractor

Objective: Talented Mortgage Broker needs to grow clientele.

Strategy: Expert Positioning

Solution(s): Increased her fees. Developed series of ongoing seminars, free information conferences, and wrote a column for magazines (hired ghost writer and licensed those available on the net).

Value Added Proposition: People wanted to work with her and seek her counsel because they were able to hear her opinions, numbers, success stories and advice prior to committing.

Method: Public speaking, free information nights and regular seminars/lunch and learns. Systemizing, recording and subsequently scripting initial consultations. She also leveraged existing joint venture with very popular real estate office.

Marketing Materials:

- Phone Script
- SWOT Analysis
- Fax Flyers
- Speakers Notes

Result: $27,245.00 profit in the first month as well as a successful business model that will be able to be licensed/sold.

Case Study Thirteen

Hockey Rink (in Australia!)

Business Type: Service-based Business

Objective: Develop a school league for a sport that was not popular or well known in the Southern Hemisphere.

Strategy: Aggressive Education

Solution(s): Developed a skating program as lead generation and beginner hockey for those interested in trying the new sport. Becoming a school sport was difficult, but the clear and obvious route for immediate and sustainable growth.

Value Added Proposition: Kids and parents were offered an alternative sport activity, and the possibility of being an elite player in a new and emerging league.

Method: Created a school league driven from the ground up through the kids (they spoke to parents... who in turn spoke to the teachers) as opposed to the school system.

Marketing Materials:
- Fundraising Program (for local schools)
- Activities Program (skating, hockey, birthday parties, sleepovers)
- Referral Program (bring a friend)

Result: A school league with over 70 (paid) teams registered and state championships.

Case Study Fourteen

Magician

Business Type: Independent Contractor

Objective: Make a profit!

Strategy: Value Added Packaging

Solution(s): A merchandise program was established to supplement the income generated from regular magic shows. Instead of relying on donations at the end of each show (like most street performers), a table was created with t-shirts and magic kits available for purchase. A salesperson was hired to man the table while the magician worked the crowd.

Value Added Proposition: Instead of a $5 donation, parents and kids could purchase $25 kits for home magic trick practice – a far better value.

Method: Table set up to sell magic kits and merchandise; salesperson was hired.

Marketing Materials:
- POS (point of sale) Material
- Magic Kits
- Uniforms + T-Shirts
- Referral Program
- Sales Training

Result: Tripled income immediately and was referred to larger paid gigs by audience members.

Case Study Fifteen

Magazine Publisher

Business Type: Independent Contractor

Objective: Find a niche market used for publishing expertise. The successful magazine publisher sold her business with a 'non-compete' clause for a high profit. She wanted to continue working and this is the only business she knew.

Strategy: Education + Expert Positioning

Solution(s): Become a consultant. Train other struggling publishing businesses how to turn a handsome profit and avoid the common pitfalls of the business.

Value Added Proposition: Publishing businesses benefit from the expertise of a former competitor, without the high salary. The high profit but high failure industry of publishing has access to a proven success.

Method: Sales letter followed by a phone call to all local publishing businesses.

- Sales Script
- Referral Program
- Sales Letter

Result: She made more in this business than she did in the last!

Case Study Sixteen

Carpet Cleaning Company

Business Type: Service-based Business

Objective: Need to increase repeat clients and reduce expense of attracting new clients.

Strategy: Client Education + Service Program

Solution(s): Most repeat clients only have their carpets cleaned every three to five years. A customer education program was created to encourage clients to increase that frequency to every six months. With hot extraction steam, the ongoing carpet cleaning program would provide health benefit for clients rather than a health detriment.

Value Added Proposition: The six-month frequency would provide clients with a health benefit, instead of a health detriment.

Method: Educate sales team and train all staff on new scripts, then create marketing material to back up claims.

Marketing Materials:
- Staff Sales Script
- Bonus Structure for Salespeople
- Marketing Collateral

Result: 27% (consistent with standard upselling statistics) of the clients bought into the program resulting in a HUGE increase in profitability.

So What Do You Do Now?

So now what?

Don't waste another minute feeling dissatisfied and overwhelmed, not getting the results you know you deserve.

Take action!

If you're already an accomplished business owner and earning in excess of $250,000.00 per year ("rich" according to the Federal Government), use this book as a resource to enhance the speed of your business success and get to the next level – multiple 7-figures. If you are not where you would like to be, then the smartest thing to do is…

A) Figure out where you are going and why you want to get there

B) Gather the tools that your business needs and engage the best team available

C) Get the help of an experienced navigator to help you define, refine and implement your strategies and reach your destination faster and more efficiently than if you were on your own

If you are serious about taking your business to the next level, then go to work on yourself, study other business successes, understand marketing strategies and become a sponge for new (proven) material. The amazing thing about the game of business is that when you put proven processes to work and continue to follow them, an abundance of success will follow.

The biggest mistake is to start off without knowing where you want to go, and being unprepared for the journey.

Get the knowledge you need to understand the course to your destination before you set sail. Think about it... if you were going to take off for distant shores, wouldn't it make sense to create a safety plan and checklist, to know the hazards of the course before you left the dock? It is amazing to me how many new (and somewhat successful) small business people set sail in business, without first gathering the necessary knowledge, tools and support to be successful. Then, when they fail, they look outward, blaming the market, the economy, their location, etc.

If you have a business and have not yet managed to create the wealth you know you deserve, the systems that allow you to take time off, build retirement accounts or pay for your children's college, then learn and master the steps outlined in this book. I am a huge advocate of education and mentorships. Get the right information, find knowledgeable, experienced support to navigate the uncharted waters, and create the quality of life you deserve.

There's no time to waste!

Learn how to avoid the 3 key mistakes all small business owners make, and get the help of an experienced Business Navigator, Mentor and Strategic Partner, visit www.businessbreakthroughpro.com.

www.ingramcontent.com/pod-product-compliance
Lightning Source LLC
Chambersburg PA
CBHW021050210326
41598CB00016B/1155